Storytelling With Sound: Fundamentals of Creative Guitar Composition

University Scholastic Press

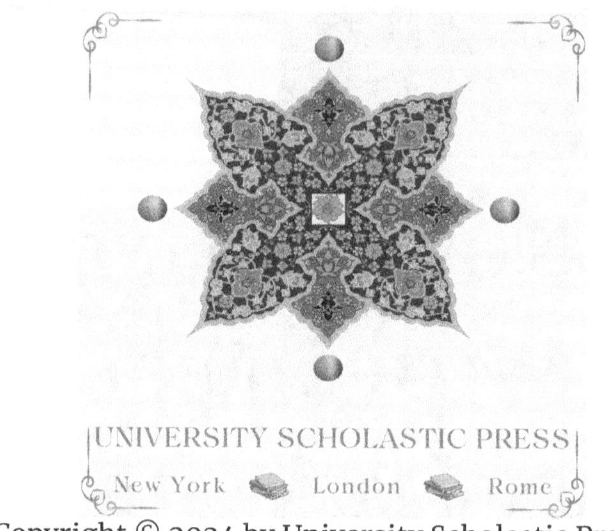

UNIVERSITY SCHOLASTIC PRESS
New York   London   Rome

Other Musician's Series Books
By University Scholastic Press:

A Guitarist's Grimoire: Unlocking the Secrets of Creating A Musical Diary To Master Guitar Composition

Storytelling With Sound: Fundamentals of Creative Guitar Composition

Musical Architecture Secrets: Structure Planning For Guitar Composition

Strings Of Brilliance: Mastering Melody and Harmony Development For Guitar Composition

Rhythm Mastery for Guitarists: Unlocking Tempo and Timing Techniques For Guitar Composition

Table Of Contents

INTRODUCTION

In the heart of every captivating melody lies a story waiting to be told. Just as a skilled author weaves words into tales that stir the imagination, a creative guitarist possesses the power to craft narratives through sound. This book is a comprehensive guide designed to unlock the boundless potential of musical expression on the six strings.

We delve deep into the art of guitar composition, offering a roadmap to navigate the vast landscape of sonic storytelling. Through a series of meticulously curated chapters, you are invited on a journey that traverses the fundamental principles of music theory, technique, and creativity.

At the outset, *Understanding Basic Chord Theory* serves as the cornerstone upon which the rest of the narrative unfolds. Here, you embark on a voyage of discovery, unraveling the mysteries of harmony and structure that underpin musical composition. From foundational concepts, the exploration expands to encompass *Chord Progressions*, *Exploring Different Keys*, and the nuanced artistry of *Using Open and Barre Chords*.

As the narrative progresses, you are introduced to the concept of *Storytelling With Sound* as a holistic approach to musical creation. Each chapter, meticulously crafted by experts in the field, serves as a building block, guiding you through essential techniques and concepts essential for musical storytelling.

Using *Chord Inversions*, *Seventh Chords and Extensions*, and *Creating Suspended and Altered Chords* offer a palette of harmonic colors, allowing you to paint vivid landscapes of sound. The exploration of *CombinIng Diatonic and Non-Diatonic Chords* further expands the horizon, blurring the lines between tradition and innovation.

With a solid foundation laid, the journey delves deeper into the realm of melodic expression. *Fingerstyle Exploration*, *Melodic Motifs and Short Phrases*, and *Understanding Mood and Theme* beckon you to go deep into the emotional tapestry of music, where every note becomes a brushstroke on the canvas of imagination.

As the narrative unfolds, emphasis is placed not only on technical proficiency but also on the cultivation of creativity and curiosity. *Listening To and Analyzing Other Musicians*, *Document Your Experiments*, and *When Experimenting, Stay Playful and Curious*, serve as guiding principles, encouraging you to embrace the spirit of exploration.

With each turn of the page, *Storytelling With Sound* empowers you to become a master narrator, wielding the guitar as a vehicle for self-expression and emotional resonance. From the intricacies of *Melodic Recording* to the art of *Refine and Simplify*, this book equips aspiring composers with the tools needed to transform musical ideas into compelling narratives.

As the journey draws to a close, *Tunings*, *Techniques*, and *Using Effects Creatively* offer a glimpse into the infinite possibilities that await the intrepid storyteller. With newfound knowledge and inspiration, you are poised to embark on their own musical odyssey, armed with the skills and confidence to craft stories that resonate with audiences far and wide.

University Scholastic Press

UNDERSTANDING BASIC CHORD THEORY

Familiarize yourself with basic chord theory, including major and minor chords, seventh chords, and extended chords. Understand the intervals and structures that make up different chord types.

Understanding basic chord theory is essential for guitar composition.

Let's dive deep! Study this concise overview of fundamental chord theory concepts that will help you in crafting your compositions.

CHORD BASICS

A chord is a group of three or more notes played simultaneously. On the guitar, chords are often formed by playing specific combinations of open strings and fretted notes.

The three primary types of chords are major, minor, and diminished. These chords have distinct sounds and emotional qualities.

Major Chords:

Major chords have a bright, happy sound.

They are typically constructed by combining the root, major third, and perfect fifth notes of a major scale.

Minor Chords:

Minor chords have a more somber, melancholic sound.

They consist of the root, minor third, and perfect fifth notes of a major scale.

Diminished Chords:

Diminished chords create tension and instability.

They are formed by combining the root, minor third, and diminished fifth notes.

Chord Progressions:

Chord progressions are sequences of chords played in a specific order. They form the harmonic structure of a composition.

Common progressions include the I–IV–V (1–4–5) progression and the ii–V–I progression.

Chord Inversions:

Chord inversions involve changing the order of notes within a chord. This can create smoother transitions between chords and add variety to your compositions.

Common inversions include root position, first inversion, and second inversion.

Barre Chords:

Barre chords allow you to play chords using the same chord shape moved along the neck.

The most common barre chords are based on the E and A chord shapes.

Seventh Chords:

Seventh chords add an extra note to the basic triad, creating a richer sound.

Common seventh chords include major 7th (maj7), dominant 7th (7), and minor 7th (m7) chords.

Extended Chords:

Extended chords go beyond the basic seventh chords and include additional notes like ninths, elevenths, and thirteenths.

These chords add complexity and color to your compositions.

Modal Chords:

Modal chords are based on modes derived from the major scale.

Common modal chords include chords built on the Ionian (major), Dorian, and Mixolydian modes.

Transposition:

Transposing chords involves changing the key of a chord progression. This can be useful for finding the optimal vocal range or adapting a composition to a different mood.

Experimentation and Voicing:

Experiment with different voicings (fingerings) of chords to discover unique sounds.

Explore open chord shapes, alternative tunings, and partial chord voicings.

Remember that these are foundational concepts, and as you progress, you may delve into more advanced harmonic theories. Developing an ear for chord progressions and understanding how different chords evoke emotions will greatly contribute to the expressiveness of your guitar compositions.

CHORD PROGRESSIONS

START WITH COMMON CHORD PROGRESSIONS

Begin by experimenting with well-known chord progressions, such as the I–IV–V progression or the ii–V–I jazz progression. These progressions provide a foundation for exploration.

There are several common chord progressions that are widely used in guitar composition across various genres. These progressions provide a foundation for creating melodies, harmonies, and building the overall structure of your compositions.

Here are some popular chord progressions:

I–IV–V (1–4–5) Progression:

This is one of the most fundamental progressions in Western music. It involves the tonic (I), subdominant (IV), and dominant (V) chords.

Example in the key of G: G – C – D.

Example in the key of C major: C – F – G

ii–V–I Jazz Progression:

Often used in jazz, this progression involves the supertonic (ii), dominant (V), and tonic (I) chords.

Example in the key of C: Dm7 – G7 – Cmaj7.

I–V–vi–IV Progression:

A widely used progression in popular music, especially in pop and rock.

Example in the key of C: C – G – Am – F.

Example in the key of G major: G – D – Em – C

vi-IV-I-V Progression:

Another common progression used in various genres, including pop and rock.

Example in the key of G: Em – C – G – D.

Example in the key of C major: Am – F – C – G

Blues Progression:

The blues progression typically follows a I–IV–V pattern, often with dominant 7th chords.

Example in the key of A: A7 – D7 – E7.

Circle of Fifths Progression:

A sequence of chords moving in intervals of fifths.

Example in the key of C: C – G – Dm – Am – E – Bdim – F – C.

Doo-Wop Progression:

A classic progression used in doo-wop and early rock and roll.

Example in the key of C: C – Am – F – G.

Sensitive Female Chord Progression:

Commonly associated with singer-songwriter and folk music.

Example in the key of G: G – Em7 – Cmaj9 – Dsus4.

Example in the key of C major: Am – F – C – G

Minor Blues Progression:

A variation of the blues progression with minor chords.

Example in the key of A: Am – Dm – E7.

Andalusian Cadence:
A distinctive progression with a descending chromatic pattern, often associated with flamenco music.
Example in the key of Am: Am – G – F – E.

Folk Progression:
Simple and versatile, used in various folk and acoustic genres.
Example in the key of D: D – G – A.

Reggae Progression:
A characteristic progression used in reggae music.
Example in the key of C: C – G – Am – F.

Pop–Punk Progression (I–V–vi–IV in various keys):
Example in the key of C major: C – G – Am – F
Example in the key of G major: G – D – Em – C
Example in the key of D major: D – A – Bm – G

Fingerstyle Folk Progression:
Example in the key of C major: C – G – Am – E

Remember, these are just starting points. The beauty of composition is in exploring and experimenting, so feel free to modify these progressions, change keys, and add your unique twists to create something that resonates with your style and emotions.

Experiment with these progressions, modify them, and combine them to suit the mood and style of your composition. The key to creating interesting and unique compositions is to explore different chord progressions, voicings, and rhythmic patterns while keeping in mind the emotional impact you want to convey.

EXPLORING DIFFERENT KEYS

EXPERIMENT WITH VARIOUS KEYS

Move beyond the common keys like C, G, and D, and explore the unique characteristics of less frequently used keys.

Understanding different keys is crucial for guitar composition as it allows you to explore diverse musical possibilities and create a wide range of emotions. Each key has its unique characteristics, and choosing the right key can greatly influence the mood of your composition.

MAJOR KEYS

C Major:

Known for its bright and pure sound, C Major is often used for compositions with an uplifting or joyful feel.

G Major:

With a slightly warmer tone, G Major is common in folk, country, and pop music.

D Major:

Offering a sense of brightness, D Major is versatile and frequently used in various genres.

MINOR KEYS

A Minor:

A natural choice for expressing melancholy or introspective emotions, A Minor is widely used in ballads and rock music.

E Minor:

Known for its versatility, E Minor is suitable for both somber and energetic compositions, often found in rock and metal genres.

D Minor:

With a darker undertone, D Minor is used for expressing drama and tension, common in classical and modern compositions.

RELATIVE MAJOR AND MINOR KEYS

Pairs of major and minor keys that share the same key signature. For example, C Major and A Minor are relative keys.

Transitioning between relative major and minor keys can create dynamic shifts in mood within a composition.

BLUES KEYS

A Blues:

Often used in blues compositions, A Blues provides a gritty and soulful sound.

E Blues:

Commonly used for blues and rock, E Blues is favored for its resonance on the guitar.

JAZZ KEYS

F Major:

Commonly used in jazz, F Major offers a rich and sophisticated sound.

Bb Major:

Another jazz favorite, Bb Major suits compositions that require a more mellow and laid-back atmosphere.

MODAL KEYS

D Dorian:

Frequently used in jazz and fusion, D Dorian has a cool and jazzy flavor.

A Mixolydian:

Popular in blues and rock, A Mixolydian provides a bluesy and laid-back vibe.

UNCOMMON KEYS

Db Major/Eb Minor:

Uncommon but can create a unique and mysterious atmosphere.

F# Major/G# Minor:

Offers a bright and vibrant sound, less common but distinctive.

CONSIDERATIONS FOR CHOOSING A KEY IN GUITAR COMPOSITION

Guitar Fingerings:

Some keys may be more comfortable to play on the guitar due to the instrument's tuning and fingerboard characteristics.

Tonal Quality:

Each key has a unique tonal quality, and the same melody or chord progression can evoke different emotions in different keys.

Vocal Range:

If your composition includes vocals, consider the range of the singer's voice and choose a key that suits it well.

Chord Voicings:

Certain keys may lend themselves to specific chord voicings or open strings, influencing the overall texture of your composition.

Experimenting with different keys allows you to discover new sounds and find the perfect tonal palette for your guitar composition. Don't hesitate to explore unconventional keys and combinations to add depth and uniqueness to your musical creations.

USING OPEN AND BARRE CHORDS

Combine open chords and barre chords to create rich and diverse progressions. Open chords offer a warm and resonant sound, while barre chords provide versatility and mobility on the fretboard.

Open and barre chords are fundamental components of guitar playing, and understanding how to use them can greatly enhance your abilities in guitar composition.

Let's explore open and barre chords and how they contribute to the richness and diversity of your compositions.

OPEN CHORDS

Open chords are played using at least one open string (unfretted) along with fretted notes.

They are usually found at the beginning of a composition or in sections where a full, open sound is desired.

Common Open Chords:
C Major: C, E, G, C, E (from low to high strings)
G Major: G, B, D, G, B, G
D Major: D, A, D, F#, A, D

Role in Composition:
Open chords create a bright and resonant sound.
Often used for chord progressions, accompaniment, and establishing tonality.

Versatility:

Open chords can be easily modified and embellished, adding nuances to your composition.

Changing between open chords can create smooth and pleasing transitions.

BARRE CHORDS

Barre chords involve using one finger to press down multiple strings across the guitar neck, effectively acting as a movable nut.

They allow you to play chords in different positions and keys.

Common Barre Chords:

Major Barre Chord: Rooted on the low E string, movable up and down the neck.

Minor Barre Chord: Similar to the major barre chord but with a flattened 3rd, creating a minor chord.

Dominant 7th Barre Chord Adds a flattened 7th to the major chord, commonly used in blues.

Role in Composition:

Barre chords provide a more substantial, full-bodied sound compared to open chords.

Essential for playing in different keys and transposing chord progressions.

Chord Progression Freedom:

Barre chords give you the flexibility to move chord progressions to different parts of the neck, expanding your composition possibilities.

Ideal for creating dynamic shifts and variations within a composition.

Expressive Techniques:

Barre chords can be embellished with slides, hammer-ons, and pull-offs, adding expressive elements to your playing.

Muting certain strings within a barre chord can create interesting textures.

COMBINING OPEN AND BARRE CHORDS

Harmonic Richness:

Integrating open and barre chords in a composition adds harmonic richness and variety.

Transitioning between open and barre chords can create a dynamic and evolving sound.

Tonality and Texture:

Open chords contribute to the overall tonality, while barre chords offer texture and depth.

Experimenting with the order and sequence of these chords can shape the emotional landscape of your composition.

Fingerstyle Exploration:

Fingerstyle techniques can be applied effectively to open and barre chords, providing intricate and melodic accompaniments.

Melody Accompaniment:

Barre chords offer the advantage of freeing up fingers to play melodies, while open chords provide a solid foundation.

In summary, understanding the characteristics and applications of open and barre chords equips you with a versatile set of tools for guitar composition. By experimenting with different chord progressions, voicings, and techniques, you can create unique and captivating compositions that showcase the expressive potential of the guitar.

USING CHORD INVERSIONS

Incorporate chord inversions to create smoother transitions between chords and add a sense of movement to your progressions.

UTILIZING CHORD INVERSIONS FOR GUITAR COMPOSITION

Chord inversions are a powerful tool in guitar composition, offering a fresh perspective on familiar chord progressions and enhancing the overall harmonic richness of your music. By understanding and incorporating chord inversions, you can create more interesting and dynamic arrangements.

Understanding Chord Inversions:

A chord inversion occurs when the root note of a chord is not the lowest-pitched note. Inversions are achieved by rearranging the order of the chord tones.

Types of Inversions:

First Inversion (1st Inv): The third of the chord becomes the lowest note.

Second Inversion (2nd Inv):The fifth of the chord becomes the lowest note.

Third Inversion (3rd Inv): The seventh (or any extended note) of the chord becomes the lowest note.

CREATING SMOOTH VOICE LEADING

Voice Leading Definition:

Voice leading refers to the smooth transition of individual chord tones between consecutive chords.

Advantage of Chord Inversions:

Inversions contribute to smoother voice leading, creating a more fluid and melodic harmonic progression.

ENHANCING MELODIC MOVEMENT

Utilizing Bass Movement:

Experiment with bass movement through inversions to add melodic interest to your composition.

A descending bass line created by using different inversions can create a compelling sense of movement.

CREATING TENSION AND RELEASE

Inversions for Tension:

Introduce inversions strategically to build tension within your composition.

Shifting to an inversion with a dissonant interval can create a moment of suspense.

Resolving with Root Position:

Resolve the tension by transitioning to a chord in root position. This provides a satisfying release and resolution.

ENHANCING FINGERSTYLE ARRANGEMENTS

Fingerstyle Techniques:

Chord inversions work well in fingerstyle arrangements, allowing you to maintain a consistent bass line while introducing variation in higher voicings.

Arpeggios and Inversions:

Incorporate arpeggios based on inversions to add complexity and texture to your fingerstyle compositions.

ADDING COLOR WITH EXTENDED CHORDS

Extended Chords:

Apply inversions to extended chords (chords with added seventh, ninth, eleventh, etc.) to create lush and colorful harmonic palettes.

Inverted Dominant Chords:

Experiment with inversions of dominant chords to add tension and intrigue, especially in genres like jazz and fusion.

TRANSPOSING CHORD PROGRESSIONS

Changing Tonal Centers:

Use inversions when transposing chord progressions to maintain smooth transitions and consistency in tonal centers.

ACCOMPANYING VOCAL OR LEAD LINES

Supporting Vocals:

When accompanying vocals or lead lines, inversions can be employed to avoid clashes with the melody and provide a harmonically rich backdrop.

EXPERIMENTING WITH DIFFERENT INVERSIONS

Voice Distribution:

Experiment with different inversions based on the distribution of chord tones across different strings and frets.

Timbral Variation:

Utilize inversions to create tonal variety. Higher inversions can offer a brighter and more shimmering sound, while lower inversions may provide warmth and depth.

RECORDING AND PRODUCTION CONSIDERATIONS

Layering and Mixing:

When recording, consider layering multiple guitar tracks with different chord inversions to create a fuller sound.

Use panning and EQ to distinguish between the various inversions in the mix.

Chord inversions open up a world of creative possibilities for guitar composition. Whether you're aiming for smooth voice leading, adding tension and release, or enhancing melodic movement, the strategic use of inversions can elevate your compositions to new heights. As you integrate inversions into your playing, you'll discover a broader sonic palette and develop a heightened sense of harmonic expression in your guitar compositions.

SEVENTH CHORDS AND EXTENSIONS

Integrate seventh chords (major 7, minor 7, dominant 7) and extended chords (9th, 11th, 13th) to add complexity and color to your progressions.

SEVENTH CHORDS AND EXTENSIONS IN GUITAR COMPOSITION

Seventh chords and extensions are powerful tools in guitar composition, adding complexity, color, and richness to your musical palette. Understanding how to incorporate these chords and extensions can elevate your compositions and provide a sophisticated harmonic backdrop.

Let's explore the world of seventh chords and extensions for guitar:

Understanding Seventh Chords:

A seventh chord is formed by adding a seventh interval on top of a triad (three-note chord).

The most common seventh chords are Major 7th, Dominant 7th, Minor 7th, and Half-Diminished 7th.

Chord Types:

Major 7th (maj7): Root - Major Third - Perfect Fifth - Major Seventh.

Dominant 7th (7): Root - Major Third - Perfect Fifth - Minor Seventh.

Minor 7th (m7): Root - Minor Third - Perfect Fifth - Minor Seventh.

Half-Diminished 7th (m7 5): Root – Minor Third – Diminished Fifth – Minor Seventh.

Extensions Beyond the Seventh:

Ninth Chords (9): Adds the ninth interval to a seventh chord.

Example: Dominant 9th (9): Root – Major Third – Perfect Fifth – Minor Seventh – Major Ninth.

Eleventh Chords (11): Incorporates the eleventh interval.

Example: Dominant 11th (11): Root – Major Third – Perfect Fifth – Minor Seventh – Major Ninth – Perfect Eleventh.

Thirteenth Chords (13): Extends to the thirteenth interval.

Example: Dominant 13th (13): Root – Major Third – Perfect Fifth – Minor Seventh – Major Ninth – Perfect Eleventh – Major Thirteenth.

BENEFITS OF SEVENTH CHORDS AND EXTENSIONS

Harmonic Richness:
Seventh chords and extensions introduce additional tones, creating a fuller and more complex harmonic texture.

Expressive Color:
Each type of seventh chord and extension imparts a distinct emotional color to the composition.

Major 7th chords can evoke a dreamy, sophisticated feel, while Dominant 7th chords add tension and drive.

Smooth Voice Leading:

The added notes in seventh chords allow for smoother voice leading between chords, enhancing the overall flow of your composition.

VOICING TECHNIQUES

Close Voicings:

Place the chord tones close together on the fretboard, creating a compact and vibrant sound.

Useful for intricate chord progressions and melodic accompaniment.

Spread Voicings:

Disperse the chord tones across a wider range, producing a more open and spacious sound.

Effective for creating sonic contrasts and emphasizing specific chord tones.

MODAL APPLICATIONS

Modal Interchange:

Utilize seventh chords and extensions to explore modal interchange, borrowing chords from parallel scales.

For example, introduce a Major 7th chord from a parallel major key to add unexpected tonal shifts.

COMMON PROGRESSIONS

ii-V-I Progression:

Often used in jazz and beyond, this progression involves the ii minor 7th, V dominant 7th, and I major 7th chords.

Turnaround Progression:

Incorporates Dominant 7th chords and their extensions to create a turnaround sequence, commonly found in blues and jazz.

EXPRESSIVE TECHNIQUES

Bending and Vibrato:

Enhance the expressiveness of seventh chords by incorporating bends and vibrato, adding character to sustained notes.

Arpeggios:

Break down seventh chords into arpeggios for melodic and soloing opportunities.

RECORDING CONSIDERATIONS

Layering:

Experiment with layering multiple guitar tracks, each featuring different voicings or inversions of seventh chords and extensions.

Acoustic and Electric Blending:

Combine the warmth of acoustic seventh chords with the electric brilliance of extended chords for a diverse sonic landscape.

Seventh chords and extensions offer a vast palette for guitar composition, allowing you to infuse your music with sophistication and emotional depth. Experiment with different voicings, explore harmonic possibilities, and embrace the expressive potential these chords bring to your compositions.

Whether you're crafting lush jazz progressions, adding tension to rock riffs, or incorporating extended harmonies into your acoustic arrangements, the world of seventh chords and extensions is a rich terrain waiting to be explored.

CREATING SUSPENDED AND ALTERED CHORDS

Experiment with suspended chords (sus2, sus4) and altered chords (augmented, diminished) to introduce tension and release in your progressions.

EXPLORING SUSPENDED AND ALTERED CHORDS IN GUITAR COMPOSITION

In guitar composition, suspended (sus) and altered chords offer a diverse palette of sounds, adding tension, resolution, and unique harmonic colors to your music.

The following covers creating and effectively using suspended and altered chords in your compositions.

Suspended (Sus) Chords:

Suspended chords replace the third with either the second (sus2) or the fourth (sus4), creating a sense of suspension and anticipation.

Creating Sus Chords:

Sus2: Form a sus2 chord by omitting the third and playing the root, second, and fifth.

Sus4: Construct a sus4 chord by replacing the third with the fourth while keeping the root and fifth.

Application:

Use sus chords to create tension that seeks resolution.

Transition between sus and major or minor chords for dynamic shifts in mood.

Altered Chords:

Altered chords involve modifying a dominant seventh chord by raising or lowering certain tones, typically the fifth, ninth, or thirteenth.

Common Alterations:

Dominant 7#5 (augmented): Raise the fifth.
Dominant 7b5 (diminished): Lower the fifth.
Dominant 7#9 (Hendrix chord): Raise the ninth.

Creating Altered Chords:

Experiment with different combinations of altered tones to discover unique chord voicings.

Application:

Altered chords are prevalent in jazz and fusion, adding complexity and dissonance.

Use them as transitional chords, leading to more stable harmonic resolutions.

COMBINING SUS AND ALTERED CHORDS

Creating Tension-Release Patterns:

Combine sus chords with altered chords to create sequences of tension and release.

For example, transition from a sus4 chord to a dominant 7#9 chord for a dramatic shift.

Smooth Transitions:

Pay attention to the movement of individual chord tones when transitioning between sus and altered chords.

Explore voice leading to create smooth and melodic chord progressions.

MODAL INTERCHANGE

Borrowing from Parallel Modes:

Experiment with modal interchange by borrowing sus and altered chords from parallel modes.

For instance, use a sus2 chord from the Dorian mode for a subtle modal shift.

FINGERSTYLE AND STRUMMING TECHNIQUES

Expressive Fingerpicking:

Utilize fingerpicking techniques to bring out the nuances of sus and altered chords.

Experiment with arpeggios and cascading patterns for added expressiveness.

Dramatic Strumming Patterns:

Use dynamic strumming patterns to emphasize the tension and release inherent in sus and altered chords.

Vary your strumming intensity to convey different emotional nuances.

LAYERING AND TEXTURE

Layering with Other Instruments:

Experiment with layering sus and altered chords with other instruments for a richer texture.

Consider using synthesizers, strings, or brass to complement the unique qualities of these chords.

RECORDING TECHNIQUES

Close Mic for Detail:

When recording, use a close-miking technique to capture the intricate details of sus and altered chords.

This is especially important to highlight the subtle tonal variations in altered chords.

Ambient Miking for Atmosphere:

Experiment with ambient miking to capture the natural resonance and space around the guitar, enhancing the atmospheric quality of sus chords.

MODULATION AND KEY CHANGES

Modulating with Altered Chords:

Explore key modulation by using altered chords as pivot points.

For instance, introduce an altered dominant chord to smoothly transition to a different key.

Contextual Harmony:

Evaluate the overall harmonic context of your composition to ensure that sus and altered chords serve the desired emotional and stylistic purpose.

Be mindful of their impact on the overall tonal landscape.

Suspended and altered chords are powerful tools for guitar composers, providing a wide range of expressive possibilities.

Whether used for creating tension, building unique progressions, or adding color to your compositions, these chords can elevate your music to new heights. Experiment with different voicings, techniques, and contexts to unlock the full potential of suspended and altered chords in your guitar compositions.

COMBINING DIATONIC AND NON-DIATONIC CHORDS

Mix diatonic chords (those within a key) with non-diatonic chords to create unexpected twists in your progressions.

BLENDING DIATONIC AND NON-DIATONIC CHORDS IN GUITAR COMPOSITION

Guitar composition is a rich terrain for harmonic exploration, and the interplay between diatonic and non-diatonic chords offers a vast array of creative possibilities.

Learning how to effectively combine these two types of chords will ensure you'll craft compelling and dynamic compositions:

UNDERSTANDING DIATONIC AND NON-DIATONIC CHORDS

Diatonic Chords:

Belonging to a specific key, diatonic chords are derived from the major or minor scale associated with that key.

In a major key, common diatonic chords include I, IV, and V, while in a minor key, i, iv, and V are typical.

Non-Diatonic Chords:

These chords involve tones outside the key's standard major or minor scale.

Examples include chromatic chords, borrowed chords from parallel keys or modes, and altered chords.

CRAFTING HARMONIC TENSION

Blend Diatonic with Borrowed Chords:

Borrow chords from parallel keys or modes to introduce tension and color.

For instance, use a chord from the parallel Dorian mode in a composition primarily in the natural minor scale.

Chromatic Movement:

Insert non-diatonic chords with chromatic movements to create heightened tension.

Gradual chromatic shifts can be powerful tools for building anticipation.

TRANSITIONAL CHORDS

Smooth Modulations:

Use non-diatonic chords as transitional elements between diatonic chords to modulate smoothly.

This technique can be particularly effective for transitioning between different sections of a composition.

Secondary Dominants:

Introduce non-diatonic chords as secondary dominants to lead to diatonic target chords.

For instance, use a V/V (secondary dominant) to lead to the dominant (V) chord in the new key.

EXPANDING HARMONIC PALETTE

Modal Interchange:

Experiment with modal interchange by borrowing chords from parallel modes.

Incorporate chords from the parallel major or minor mode to add unexpected colors to your composition.

Augmented and Diminished Chords:

Include augmented or diminished chords for unique harmonic textures.

These chords can serve as points of tension or provide a sense of resolution when used thoughtfully.

RHYTHMIC DYNAMICS

Syncopation and Accentuation:

Use rhythmic variations to emphasize the impact of non-diatonic chords.

Syncopated rhythms or accented strums can draw attention to these chords, creating a dynamic rhythmic interplay.

VOICE LEADING

Smooth Transitions:

Pay attention to voice leading when moving between diatonic and non-diatonic chords.

Smooth voice leading can maintain coherence and create a seamless harmonic flow.

EXPERIMENTING WITH GENRES

Jazz and Fusion Influence:

Draw inspiration from jazz and fusion genres, where the blending of diatonic and non-diatonic chords is commonplace.

Experiment with extended and altered chords for added complexity.

Blues Progressions:

Infuse blues progressions with non-diatonic chords for a modern twist.

Consider using chromatic passing chords to connect diatonic chords in a blues context.

CONTEXTUAL AWARENESS

Serving the Composition:

Evaluate the emotional and stylistic impact of introducing non-diatonic chords.

Ensure that these chords enhance the overall narrative of your composition rather than detracting from it.

LAYERING AND TEXTURE

Orchestration and Arrangement:

Experiment with orchestrating non-diatonic chords across multiple instruments or guitar voicings.

This can add depth and texture to your composition.

EXPRESSIVE TECHNIQUES

Guitar Effects:

Explore the use of guitar effects to enhance the character of non-diatonic chords.

Reverb, delay, or modulation effects can contribute to the atmospheric quality of these chords.

The fusion of diatonic and non-diatonic chords in guitar composition opens the door to innovation and emotional richness. By understanding their individual characteristics and experimenting with various harmonic techniques, you can create compositions that resonate with complexity and depth. Whether you're aiming for subtle harmonic nuances or bold, unexpected shifts, the artful combination of diatonic and non-diatonic chords can elevate your guitar compositions to new heights.

EXPLORING CHROMATIC MOVEMENT

Experiment with chromatic movements between chords. Introduce chromatic passing chords or create tension and resolution using chromatic approaches.

EXPLORING CHROMATIC MOVEMENT IN GUITAR COMPOSITION

Chromatic movement involves the use of consecutive half steps, seamlessly connecting pitches irrespective of their diatonic relationship. Integrating chromaticism into your guitar compositions can add a layer of tension, excitement, and unpredictability.

Let's explore chromatic movement further so you may incorporate this technique effectively into your guitar composition.

UNDERSTANDING CHROMATICISM

Chromatic vs. Diatonic:

Diatonic movement follows the notes within a specific key or scale.

Chromatic movement involves using all twelve pitches, including sharps and flats, to create a more expansive and dynamic sound.

ADDING TENSION AND RELEASE

Creating Dissonance:

Chromaticism introduces dissonance, creating tension within your composition.

Utilize chromatic passages to build anticipation and prepare for resolving to more stable harmonies.

Resolving Chromatic Tension:

Resolve chromatic movements to consonant tones or chords for a satisfying release.

This contrast enhances the emotional impact of your composition.

EXPLORING DIFFERENT CHROMATIC TECHNIQUES

Chromatic Scales:

Experiment with ascending and descending chromatic scales, both as single-note passages and incorporated into chords.

Chromatic Passing Tones:

Insert chromatic passing tones between diatonic scale degrees to add color and flair to your melodies or harmonies.

Chromatic Chord Progressions:

Create unique chord progressions by introducing chromatic chords that provide unexpected twists in your composition.

INTEGRATING CHROMATICISM IN MELODIES

Sliding Techniques:

Use slides to smoothly connect chromatic notes, adding a fluid and expressive quality to your melodies.

Hammer-Ons and Pull-Offs:

Employ hammer-ons and pull-offs to execute rapid chromatic passages, enhancing the virtuosity of your playing.

CHROMATIC HARMONY

Altered Chords:

Incorporate altered chords with chromatic notes, such as augmented or diminished chords, to introduce sophisticated harmonic nuances.

Modal Interchange:

Use chromaticism to explore modal interchange, borrowing chords from parallel scales to introduce fresh and unexpected harmonic colors.

CHROMATIC MOVEMENT IN CHORD PROGRESSIONS

Chromatic Mediants:

Explore chromatic mediant relationships between chords for a dramatic shift in tonality.

Chromatic Descending Basslines:

Introduce chromaticism in descending basslines to create a sense of gravity and depth in your chord progressions.

DYNAMIC RHYTHMIC CHROMATICISM

Stutter-Step Rhythms:

Apply chromatic passages with staggered rhythms for a dynamic and unpredictable rhythmic feel.

Syncopated Chromatic Hits:

Use syncopation with chromatic notes to emphasize specific beats and create rhythmic tension.

CHROMATICISM IN BLUES AND JAZZ

Bluesy Chromatic Runs:

Infuse your compositions with bluesy chromatic runs, especially effective in blues and jazz-influenced styles.

Bebop Chromaticism:

Emulate the bebop style by incorporating fast and fluid chromatic runs, adding sophistication to your improvisations.

CONTRASTING DIATONIC AND CHROMATIC ELEMENTS

Strategic Placement:

Use chromaticism strategically to contrast with diatonic elements, emphasizing specific musical phrases or sections.

RECORDING AND PRODUCTION TIPS

Layering Chromatic Passages:

When recording, experiment with layering multiple guitar tracks featuring different chromatic passages for a fuller and more textured sound.

Effect Processing:

Enhance the impact of chromatic movements with effects like reverb or delay to create a sense of space and atmosphere.

Chromatic movement is a versatile tool that can add flair, tension, and emotional depth to your guitar compositions. Whether used in melodies, harmonies, or chord progressions, the judicious application of chromaticism can elevate your music to new levels of expressiveness. As you explore and integrate chromatic elements into your guitar compositions, you'll discover a rich and vibrant palette of sonic possibilities that can captivate and engage your listeners.

CREATING MODAL PROGRESSIONS

Experiment with modal chord progressions, such as those found in modes like **Dorian**, **Phrygian**, or **Mixolydian**. This adds a distinctive flavor to your compositions.

CREATING MODAL PROGRESSIONS FOR GUITAR COMPOSITION

Modal progressions offer a unique and colorful approach to guitar composition, allowing you to explore diverse tonalities beyond the conventional major and minor keys. Understanding modal harmony can open up new avenues for creativity and expression.

Let's look at how we can create modal progressions for your guitar compositions:

UNDERSTANDING MODES

Modal Basics:
Modes are scales derived from a parent scale, each with its distinct set of intervals and characteristic sound.
Common modes include Ionian, Dorian, Phrygian, Lydian, Mixolydian, Aeolian, and Locrian.

IDENTIFYING MODAL CHARACTERISTICS

Ionian (Major):
Bright and uplifting, suitable for conveying a sense of positivity.

Root, Major 2nd, Major 3rd, Perfect 4th, Perfect 5th, Major 6th, Major 7th.

Dorian:

Jazzier and bluesy, with a minor seventh that adds a touch of tension.

Root, Major 2nd, Minor 3rd, Perfect 4th, Perfect 5th, Major 6th, Minor 7th.

Phrygian:

Exotic and Spanish-flavored, characterized by a minor second interval.

Root, Minor 2nd, Minor 3rd, Perfect 4th, Perfect 5th, Minor 6th, Minor 7th.

Lydian:

Ethereal and dreamy, featuring a raised fourth that creates a sense of floating.

Root, Major 2nd, Major 3rd, Augmented 4th, Perfect 5th, Major 6th, Major 7th.

Mixolydian:

Bluesy and rock-oriented, distinguished by a dominant seventh.

Root, Major 2nd, Major 3rd, Perfect 4th, Perfect 5th, Major 6th, Minor 7th.

Aeolian (Natural Minor):

Dark and emotive, akin to the natural minor scale.

Root, Major 2nd, Minor 3rd, Perfect 4th, Perfect 5th, Minor 6th, Minor 7th.

Locrian:

Unstable and dissonant, rarely used as a standalone mode.

Root, Minor 2nd, Minor 3rd, Perfect 4th, Diminished 5th, Minor 6th, Minor 7th.

CRAFTING MODAL PROGRESSIONS

Choose a Modal Center:

Select a mode to serve as the **tonal center** for your progression.

For instance, if you choose D Dorian, your **tonal center** is D, and the characteristic intervals of the Dorian mode apply.

Experiment with Chord Qualities:

Use triads, seventh chords, or extended chords that align with the chosen mode's intervals.

Dorian might involve minor and minor seventh chords, while Lydian could feature major and major seventh chords.

Modal Interchange:

Experiment with modal interchange by borrowing chords from parallel modes.

For example, introducing a chord from D Mixolydian while in D Dorian can create an interesting tonal shift.

COMMON MODAL PROGRESSIONS

Dorian Blues Progression:

In D Dorian: Dm7 – G7 – Dm7 – A7.

Embrace the bluesy character of Dorian with minor and dominant seventh chords.

Lydian Dream Sequence:

In A Lydian: AMaj7 – Bm7 – GMaj7 – F#m7
Explore the dreamy, floating quality of Lydian with major seventh chords.

Mixolydian Rock Groove:

In E Mixolydian: E7 – A7 – Bm7.
Capture the rock–oriented vibe of Mixolydian with dominant seventh chords.

MELODIC AND SOLOING OPPORTUNITIES

Leverage Modal Scale Patterns:

Learn the unique scale patterns associated with each mode to create melodic lines and solos.

Modal Targeting:

Highlight characteristic tones of each mode during solos to emphasize the distinct modal flavor.

RECORDING AND PRODUCTION TIPS

Layering and Textures:

Experiment with layering different guitars playing chords and melodies in different modes to create rich textures.

Effects and Atmosphere:

Use effects such as reverb and delay to enhance the atmospheric quality of modal progressions.

Creating modal progressions for guitar composition opens up a world of sonic possibilities. Experiment with different modes, chord qualities, and modal interchange to infuse your compositions with unique tonal colors.

Whether you're aiming for a bluesy Dorian feel, an ethereal Lydian soundscape, or a rock-inspired Mixolydian groove, modal progressions provide a versatile palette for your creative expression on the guitar.

RHYTHMIC PATTERNS EXPERIMENTATION

Vary the rhythmic patterns within your chord progressions. Explore different strumming patterns, arpeggios, and syncopations.

EXPLORING DYNAMIC AND INNOVATIVE RHYTHMIC PATTERNS IN GUITAR COMPOSITION

Rhythmic patterns are the heartbeat of a guitar composition, shaping its character and providing a foundation for expressive musicality. Experimenting with rhythmic elements can breathe life into your compositions, creating dynamic energy and enhancing the overall listening experience.

FOUNDATION OF RHYTHMIC PATTERNS

Understanding Meter and Time Signatures:
Familiarize yourself with different meters and time signatures to establish the foundational structure of your composition.

Experiment with common time signatures like 4/4, 3/4, or explore unconventional ones for a unique rhythmic feel.

Tempo Exploration:
Adjust the tempo to influence the mood and energy of your composition.

Experiment with both slow and fast tempos to discover how they impact the overall rhythmic flow.

DYNAMIC STRUMMING AND PICKING

Strumming Variations:

Vary your strumming patterns to create different rhythmic textures.

Experiment with techniques like palm muting, percussive strumming, and directional strumming for diverse rhythmic effects.

Fingerstyle Dynamics:

Explore fingerpicking techniques with varying patterns.

Experiment with alternating bass notes, arpeggios, and fingerstyle percussive elements to add depth to your rhythmic palette.

SYNCOPATION AND OFFBEAT ACCENTS

Syncopated Rhythms:

Introduce syncopation by emphasizing offbeats.

Experiment with syncopated strumming or picking patterns to create a sense of rhythmic tension and excitement.

Offbeat Accents:

Place accents on unexpected beats or offbeats to break away from predictable patterns.

This can add a layer of unpredictability and interest to your composition.

Polyrhythms and Cross-Rhythms

Polyrhythmic Exploration:

Experiment with polyrhythms by layering contrasting rhythmic patterns.

Create tension and complexity by combining different meters simultaneously.

Cross-Rhythmic Patterns:

Introduce cross-rhythms where different subdivisions conflict with each other.

This technique can result in intricate and engaging rhythmic interactions.

Time Signature Changes

Dynamism through Changes:

Incorporate changes in time signatures within your composition.

Transitioning between time signatures can bring a sense of surprise and uniqueness to your rhythmic landscape.

Percussive Elements

Body Percussion and Tapping:

Utilize the guitar as a percussive instrument by incorporating tapping on the body or strings.

This adds rhythmic complexity and provides a percussive layer to your composition.

Percussive Striking:

Experiment with percussive striking of the strings while muting them for a rhythmic, drum-like effect.

This technique can be particularly effective in acoustic compositions.

EXPERIMENTING WITH ODD METERS

Odd Time Signatures:

Venture into odd time signatures (e.g., 5/4, 7/8) for a distinctive rhythmic feel.

Experiment with subdividing these meters to create interesting rhythmic patterns.

DRUM PATTERN INSPIRATION

Drum Groove Imitation:

Draw inspiration from drum patterns to shape your guitar rhythms.

Experiment with imitating drum grooves or creating complementary patterns.

LAYERING AND TEXTURING

Rhythmic Layering:

Layer different rhythmic patterns to create complexity.

Consider assigning different rhythmic responsibilities to different instruments or guitar parts for a textured sound.

EMOTIONAL RHYTHM

Match Rhythm to Emotion:

Align your rhythmic choices with the emotional tone of your composition.

Experiment with how subtle or intense rhythms can evoke different feelings.

Experimentation is the key to discovering unique rhythmic patterns that define your signature sound. Whether you're exploring intricate fingerstyle arrangements, experimenting with odd meters, or incorporating percussive elements, rhythmic innovation opens up a world of creative possibilities.

By continuously pushing boundaries and seeking inspiration from various genres and techniques, you can infuse your guitar compositions with dynamic rhythms that captivate and resonate with your audience.

University Scholastic Press

LISTENING TO AND ANALYZING OTHER MUSICIANS

Listen to a variety of music and analyze the styles and techniques used by other musicians. Take inspiration from different genres and adapt elements to your own style.

QUESTIONS TO CONSIDER AS YOU FIND INSPIRATION FROM OTHER MUSICIANS

When listening to and analyzing other musicians to inspire your own guitar compositions, consider asking yourself the following questions:

What Emotional Impact Does the Music Have?

Identify the emotions evoked by the music. How does the artist convey and amplify emotions through their composition?

How is the Melody Crafted?

Analyze the structure of the melody. Is it simple or intricate? How does the melody interact with the harmony, and what makes it memorable?

What Chord Progressions Are Used?

Explore the chord progressions employed in the music. How do they contribute to the overall mood? Are there unexpected or unique chord changes?

How is Rhythm Utilized?

Focus on the rhythmic elements. Is there a distinctive rhythm that drives the composition? How do variations in rhythm contribute to the overall feel?

What Techniques Stand Out?

Pay attention to the guitarist's techniques. Are there specific picking patterns, fingerstyle techniques, or unique playing styles that catch your ear?

What Role Does Dynamics Play?

Consider the use of dynamics (volume variations) in the composition. How do changes in volume enhance the overall dynamics and emotional impact?

Is There a Storytelling Element?

Determine if there's a narrative or storytelling element in the music. How does the artist convey a sense of storytelling through their composition?

How Are Different Sections Connected?

Examine how various sections of the composition are connected. Are there smooth transitions between verses, choruses, and bridges?

What is the Role of Harmony?

Analyze how harmony is used. Are there complex harmonies, or is the composition more focused on simple and effective chord progressions?

What is the Role of Silence and Pauses?

Take note of the use of silence and pauses. How does the artist leverage moments of quiet or absence of sound for dramatic effect?

Is There a Unique Sound or Timbre?

Explore the overall sound and timbre. Does the artist have a signature tone or sonic quality that sets them apart?

How Do Different Instruments Interact?

If the composition involves multiple instruments, observe how they interact. How is the synergy between guitar and other instruments achieved?

What is the Overall Structure?

Consider the overall structure of the composition. How is it organized, and does it follow a traditional or more unconventional structure?

Does the Music Tell a Cultural Story?

If applicable, explore whether the music reflects a particular cultural influence. How does cultural context contribute to the composition?

How Does the Artist Engage the Audience?

Consider how the artist engages the audience. What elements make the composition accessible or captivating for listeners?

What Can I Learn and Adapt to My Style?

Reflect on what aspects of the music inspire you. How can you adapt certain techniques, approaches, or concepts to your own guitar compositions?

Listening and analyzing with a critical ear will deepen your understanding of different musical elements and styles, providing valuable insights for your own creative process.

DOCUMENT YOUR EXPERIMENTS

Keep a musical diary. Document the techniques, styles and progressions you create, note what you like about them, and use them as a reference for future compositions.

A musical diary is a tool that allows you to document and organize various styles you come across, create, or experiment with. Keeping a musical diary can be beneficial for musicians, especially guitarists, as it serves as a reference and source of inspiration for future compositions.

You can create an all-encompassing musical diary or several individualized diaries to single out various techniques or styles, focusing on things like melody, harmonics or rhythms.

As an example, let's set up a musical diary just to document chord progressions.

SETTING UP A CHORD PROGRESSION MUSICAL DIARY

Physical or Digital Format:

Decide whether you prefer a physical journal (notebook, binder) or a digital format (document, spreadsheet, dedicated app). Choose a format that suits your preferences and is easily accessible.

Sections and Categories:

Divide your journal into sections or categories based on your preferences. You might organize it by musical genre, mood, or create sections for different tempos and styles.

Entry Format:

Standardize the format for each entry. Include key information such as the chord progression, tempo, time signature, and any specific notes or observations about the progression.

ELEMENTS TO INCLUDE IN YOUR CHORD PROGRESSION JOURNAL

Chord Progression:

Write down the chord progression using chord symbols (e.g., C, G, Am, F). Include both the chords and their sequence in the progression.

Rhythm and Strumming Pattern:

Note the rhythm and strumming pattern associated with the chord progression. This adds a layer of detail that can be crucial when recreating the progression later.

Key and Mode:

Specify the key of the chord progression and, if applicable, the mode (major, minor, Dorian, etc.). This information provides context for the harmonic content.

Tempo and Time Signature:

Include the tempo (BPM) and time signature of the progression. This is important for understanding the rhythmic structure.

Song Reference:

If the chord progression is from a specific song, mention the song title and artist. This makes it easy to revisit the original context later.

Instrumentation:

Specify if the progression is intended for a specific instrument or combination of instruments. For guitarists, you might note if the progression is fingerpicked, strummed, or a combination.

Mood or Emotion:

Record the mood or emotion conveyed by the progression. This can be subjective but helps you recall the intended feeling when revisiting the progression.

Date and Source:

Include the date you added the progression to your journal. If the progression is from a specific source or influenced by another musician, note that information.

Additional Notes:

Leave space for any additional observations or notes about the progression. This could include thoughts on how to modify or adapt the progression for your own compositions.

USING YOUR CHORD PROGRESSION JOURNAL

Inspiration Source:

When looking for inspiration for a new composition, flip through your journal. You might find a chord progression that sparks creativity.

Experimentation Playground:

Use the journal as a space to experiment with modifications or combinations of existing progressions. This can lead to the creation of unique progressions.

Educational Resource:

If you're learning about music theory, your journal can serve as an educational resource. Analyze progressions to understand their theoretical underpinnings.

Collaboration Tool:

If you collaborate with other musicians, share your chord progression journal to exchange ideas and incorporate diverse influences into your compositions.

Remember, your musical diary is a personal tool, so feel free to adapt and customize it based on your needs and preferences. The goal is to create a resource that enhances your creativity and aids your musical journey.

WHEN EXPERIMENTING, STAY PLAYFUL AND CURIOUS

Approach experimentation with a playful and curious mindset. Don't be afraid to make mistakes or try unconventional ideas.

THE JOURNEY AND THE DESTINATION

Don't rush and have fun while experimenting with guitar composition. A 'nothing is off-limits' attitude is essential for fostering creativity.

Let outline various ways and methods to keep the creative process enjoyable and explorative.

Freeform Jamming:

Set aside dedicated time for freeform jamming. Play without a specific goal, letting your fingers explore the fretboard. This can lead to unexpected and innovative chord progressions.

Improvise Regularly:

Incorporate regular improvisation sessions into your practice routine. Improvising helps you stay in the moment, allowing spontaneous ideas to emerge.

Explore Unconventional Tunings:

Experiment with alternative guitar tunings. Unconventional tunings can inspire fresh ideas and force you to approach composition from a different perspective.

Use Guitar Effects:

Incorporate various guitar effects pedals to manipulate your sound. Experiment with delay, reverb, modulation, and other effects to create unique textures and atmospheres.

Play Different Genres:

Step out of your comfort zone and explore different musical genres. Incorporate elements from genres you wouldn't typically play to add diversity to your compositions.

Mood Boards and Visual Inspiration:

Create mood boards or gather visual inspiration. Images, artwork, or even scenes from nature can spark creative ideas and guide the mood of your compositions.

Collaborate with Other Musicians:

Collaborate with musicians from diverse backgrounds. Working with others introduces new perspectives and ideas, keeping the process dynamic and exciting.

Challenge Yourself:

Set challenges for yourself. For example, compose a piece using only a specific set of chords or a certain tempo. Challenges fuel creativity.

Experiment with Non-Guitar Sounds:

Incorporate non-guitar sounds into your compositions. This could include incorporating found sounds, samples, or using your guitar in unconventional ways.

Songwriting Games:

Play songwriting games to break routine. For example, randomly select chords, time signatures, or keys, and challenge yourself to create a composition using those elements.

Reverse Engineering:

Reverse engineer songs you enjoy. Analyze chord progressions, melodies, and structures. This analytical approach can lead to innovative combinations in your own compositions.

Fingerstyle and Percussive Techniques:

Explore fingerstyle and percussive techniques on the guitar. These techniques can add a rhythmic and dynamic dimension to your compositions.

Write in Different Environments:

Change your writing environment. Write outdoors, in a different room, or even in a public space. A change of scenery can stimulate creativity.

Musical Prompts:

Use prompts to inspire compositions. Create a list of words, emotions, or concepts, and randomly select one as a starting point for your next composition.

Record and Listen Back:

Record your improvisations and compositions. Listening back allows you to identify interesting moments, ideas, or happy accidents that you might want to explore further.

Attend Workshops and Masterclasses:

Attend guitar workshops or masterclasses to learn new techniques and approaches. Exposure to different teaching styles can ignite curiosity and playful exploration.

Study Unconventional Artists:

Explore the works of unconventional or avant-garde artists. Their approaches can challenge traditional norms and inspire you to think outside the box.

Mindful Practice:

Practice mindfulness while playing. Focus on the physical sensations, the sound, and the emotions you're expressing. This mindful approach can lead to more intentional and inspired compositions.

The key is to maintain a sense of curiosity, playfulness, and openness to experimentation. Embrace the joy of discovery as you explore the vast possibilities of guitar composition.

FINGERSTYLE EXPLORATION

Fngerstyle techniques allow for intricate and expressive playing.

You may want to explore new fingerings and approaches tailored to specific tunings and techniques.

For instance, slide guitar is well-suited to alternate tunings, such as Open D or Open G. Experiment with slide techniques to add a bluesy or folk-inspired flavor to your composition.

One of the captivating aspects of guitar playing is the ability to blend different techniques, creating a rich and dynamic sound.

Experiment with different playing techniques, including fingerpicking and strumming. The choice of technique can significantly impact the mood and texture of your chord progressions.

Let's dive into how to effectively integrate fingerpicking and strumming for expressive and engaging guitar compositions.

UNDERSTANDING FINGERPICKING AND STRUMMING

Fingerpicking:

Involves plucking individual strings with your fingers, typically using the thumb, index, middle, and ring fingers.

Enables intricate melodic patterns, arpeggios, and nuanced control over dynamics.

Strumming:

Involves sweeping the pick across multiple strings simultaneously.

Ideal for creating a percussive and rhythmic foundation, commonly used in various genres like folk, pop, and rock.

CHOOSING SECTIONS FOR EACH TECHNIQUE

Intro and Verse:

Use fingerpicking for softer, more delicate sections, introducing melodic nuances and intricate patterns.

This creates an intimate atmosphere, drawing listeners into the composition.

Chorus and Bridge:

Incorporate strumming for dynamic and powerful sections. This adds energy and intensity to the composition, making it more impactful during climactic moments.

HYBRID PICKING

Combine Techniques Simultaneously:

Experiment with hybrid picking, where you use a pick for strumming and fingers for picking simultaneously.

This technique allows for a seamless transition between strummed chords and picked melodies within the same passage.

DYNAMIC CONTRAST

Striking a Balance:

Utilize the contrast between the soft, intricate fingerpicked sections and the bold, rhythmic strumming.

This creates a dynamic listening experience, keeping the audience engaged throughout the composition.

CHORD PROGRESSIONS

Fingerpicked Arpeggios:

Choose fingerpicked arpeggios for chord progressions in the verses. This provides a melodic, introspective quality.

Strummed Chords:

Use strummed chords for powerful, full-bodied progressions in the chorus. Strumming adds depth and drives the composition forward.

TRANSITIONS

Smooth Transitioning:

Ensure smooth transitions between fingerpicking and strumming sections.

Gradual shifts in intensity and dynamics help maintain cohesion in your composition.

EMOTIONAL EXPRESSION

Fingerpicking for Emotion:

Use fingerpicking to convey emotional depth and subtlety, allowing for nuanced expression in softer, reflective moments.

Strumming for Impact:

Employ strumming to add impact and intensity to climactic sections, enhancing the emotional resonance of your composition.

MELODY INTEGRATION

Fingerpicked Melodies:

Integrate fingerpicked melodies into strummed sections to add a layer of complexity and capture listeners' attention.

Strumming with Melodic Elements:

Infuse melodic elements into strummed sections, creating a harmonious blend of rhythm and lead.

RHYTHMIC PATTERNS

Fingerstyle Rhythms:

Develop rhythmic patterns in fingerpicking that complement the overall rhythm of your composition.

Strumming Dynamics:

Experiment with varying strumming dynamics to inject rhythmic diversity and maintain listener interest.

RECORDING TECHNIQUES

Separate Tracks for Clarity:

Consider recording fingerpicking and strumming parts on separate tracks during production for greater control over the mix.

Panning and Stereo Effects:

Use panning and stereo effects to create spatial separation between fingerpicked and strummed elements, enhancing the auditory experience.

Combining fingerpicking and strumming in your guitar compositions provides a broad spectrum of tonal possibilities. By strategically incorporating these techniques based on the emotional and dynamic needs of your composition, you can create a captivating and well-rounded musical experience.

Whether crafting delicate intros or powerful choruses, the synergy of fingerpicking and strumming adds depth, texture, and expressiveness to your guitar compositions.

MELODIC MOTIFS AND SHORT PHRASES

Creating melodic motifs or short phrases is a key aspect of crafting memorable and expressive compositions on the guitar.

MELODIC IDEAS

There are several reasons why melodic motifs and short phrases play a crucial role in capturing the essence of guitar composition -- let's explore!

Memorability:

Melodic motifs are memorable musical phrases that listeners can easily recall. By incorporating catchy and distinctive motifs, you create a musical identity for your composition, making it more likely to stick in the minds of your audience.

Expressiveness:

Short phrases allow for focused expression. A well-crafted motif can convey a specific emotion or theme concisely, providing a powerful means of expressing your musical ideas with precision and impact.

Structural Significance:

Melodic motifs often serve as structural elements within a composition. They can mark the beginning or end of a section, act as a recurring theme, or serve as a musical anchor that ties the piece together.

Listener Engagement:

Engaging melodies capture the listener's attention. Short phrases and motifs act as musical hooks, drawing the audience into the composition and creating a sense of anticipation for their return.

Unity and Cohesion:

Melodic motifs contribute to the unity and cohesion of a composition. When recurring throughout the piece, motifs create a sense of continuity, connecting different sections and providing a thread that weaves the musical narrative together.

Variety and Interest:

By using a variety of melodic motifs, you introduce interest and diversity into your composition. Different motifs can represent contrasting emotions, moods, or musical ideas, enhancing the overall richness of the piece.

Narrative Development:

Melodic motifs can contribute to the development of a musical narrative. Like characters in a story, motifs can evolve, transform, or reappear in different contexts, guiding the listener through a dynamic and evolving musical journey.

Interaction with Harmony:

Melodic motifs often interact with underlying harmonies and chord progressions. This interaction creates a harmonically rich and layered composition, as the melodic elements complement and enhance the harmonic structure.

Emotional Impact:

Short and focused melodic phrases have the power to evoke specific emotions. Whether joyful, melancholic, or suspenseful, well-crafted motifs contribute to the emotional impact of the composition, resonating with the listener on a deeper level.

Recognition and Signature:

Iconic melodic motifs can become a signature element of a composition or even an artist's style. Think of these motifs as musical signatures that listeners associate with your work, contributing to your unique musical identity.

In summary, melodic motifs and short phrases are essential tools in crafting a compelling and resonant guitar composition. They enhance memorability, expressiveness, and structural integrity while fostering listener engagement and contributing to the overall unity and richness of the musical experience.

UNDERSTANDING MOOD AND THEME

Clarify the mood or theme you want to convey in your composition. Consider the emotional tone and atmosphere you aim to create.

Understanding the mood and theme is a fundamental aspect of crafting a compelling guitar composition. The mood sets the emotional tone of the piece, while the theme provides a central idea or concept that guides the creative process.

Let's explore how you can approach understanding and incorporating mood and theme into your guitar compositions.

UNDERSTANDING MOOD

Identify Emotions:

Consider the emotions you want to convey through your composition. Is it a joyful, melancholic, triumphant, or contemplative piece? Define the primary emotional content you aim to express.

Explore Dynamics:

Experiment with dynamics to influence the mood. Soft, gentle passages may evoke introspection, while bold and dynamic sections can convey excitement or intensity.

Utilize Timbre and Tone:

Explore different timbres and tones on the guitar to enhance the emotional impact. For example, warm, sustained chords may create a comforting mood, while crisp, staccato notes can add tension.

Consider Tempo:

The tempo of your composition plays a crucial role in establishing mood. A slow tempo often conveys a reflective or pensive mood, while a fast tempo can evoke energy and enthusiasm.

Use Modalities:

Experiment with different musical modes to influence mood. Major modes tend to sound bright and uplifting, while minor modes often convey a sense of melancholy or introspection.

UNDERSTANDING THEME

Define the Central Idea:

Clearly define the central idea or theme you want your composition to revolve around. It could be inspired by a personal experience, a story, nature, or any concept that resonates with you.

Create Musical Narratives:

If your composition tells a story, align the musical elements with the narrative. Different sections can represent plot points, characters, or moods within the overarching theme.

Use Symbolism:

Incorporate symbolic musical elements that represent aspects of your theme. This could involve recurring motifs, specific chord progressions, or stylistic choices that embody the essence of your chosen theme.

Experiment with Genres:

Explore different musical genres that align with your theme. Genres often have associated conventions and tonal characteristics that can enhance the expression of your chosen theme.

Connect Mood and Theme:

Ensure that the mood and theme are in harmony. The emotional tone should complement and reinforce the central idea, creating a cohesive and impactful musical experience.

Consider Your Audience:

Reflect on how your chosen theme and mood will resonate with your target audience. Consider whether your composition is intended for personal expression, entertainment, or a specific message.

BRINGING IT TOGETHER

Balance and Contrast:

Strive for a balance between consistency and variety in mood and theme. Introduce contrast when needed to keep the composition engaging and dynamic.

Personal Connection:

Infuse your personal experiences and emotions into the composition. A genuine connection to the mood and theme enhances authenticity and resonance.

Revisit and Revise:

Throughout the composition process, revisit your initial ideas about mood and theme. Be open to revisions that strengthen the alignment between your creative vision and the musical realization.

Understanding the mood and theme provides a strong foundation for your guitar composition, guiding creative decisions and ensuring a coherent and expressive musical journey.

IDENTIFYING KEY MELODIC ELEMENTS

Determine key melodic elements that align with your composition's essence. Are you aiming for a lyrical, rhythmic, or atmospheric melody?

MELODIC DEPTH

Melodic elements play a crucial role in shaping the character and emotional impact of a guitar composition.

Here is a short list of key melodic elements to consider when crafting your guitar pieces.

Melodic Phrasing:

Develop distinctive and memorable melodic phrases. Pay attention to the rhythm, contour, and shape of your melodic lines.

Motifs and Themes:

Create recurring motifs or themes that serve as recognizable musical elements throughout the composition. These can be short musical ideas that contribute to cohesion.

Intervallic Movement:

Experiment with different intervals to add variety and interest to your melodies. Explore leaps, steps, and repetitions to create movement and tension.

Scalar Patterns:

Use scales to create melodic patterns. Ascending or descending scales can be employed to convey different emotions and add a sense of direction to your melodies.

Chromaticism:

Introduce chromatic notes for color and expressiveness. Chromatic passages can add tension or create unexpected twists in your melodic lines.

Grace Notes and Ornaments:

Incorporate grace notes, trills, slides, or other ornaments to embellish your melodies. These details can add flair and intricacy to your melodic phrases.

Dynamic Variation:

Experiment with dynamic changes within your melodies. Varying the volume and intensity adds nuance and emotion to your melodic lines.

Use of Rests:

Silence and pauses are as important as sound. Use rests strategically to create space and emphasize certain moments in your melodies.

Arpeggios:

Employ arpeggios to outline chords melodically. This technique adds a harmonic dimension to your melody, creating a connection with the underlying chords.

Bending and Vibrato:

Utilize bending and vibrato techniques to infuse expressiveness into your melodies. These techniques can add warmth and character to individual notes.

Modal Exploration:

Explore different musical modes to evoke specific moods. Modal melodies can contribute to the overall atmosphere of your composition.

Call and Response:

Introduce call-and-response patterns within your melodies. This involves creating a musical question (call) followed by an answer (response), enhancing the conversational quality of your composition.

Counterpoint:

Experiment with counterpoint by introducing multiple melodic lines that interact harmonically. This technique can add complexity and richness to your compositions.

Melodic Climax:

Build towards melodic climaxes or high points in your composition. This creates a sense of progression and emotional intensity.

Adaptability:

Ensure that your melodic elements are adaptable to different sections of your composition. Consider how melodic ideas can be transformed or developed over the course of the piece.

Emotional Resonance:

Ultimately, aim for emotional resonance. Craft melodies that connect with the listener on an emotional level, conveying the intended mood and theme of your composition.

As you work with these melodic elements, consider how they interact with the harmonic and rhythmic aspects of your composition. Balancing these elements contributes to a well-rounded and engaging guitar piece.

EXPERIMENT WITH SCALE CHOICES

Choose a scale or mode that complements your composition's mood. Major and minor scales are common, but exploring modes like Dorian or Mixolydian can add unique flavors.

COMMON WHOLE AND HALF STEP SCALES

(W = Whole step, H = Half step)

Major Scale:
W–W–H–W–W–W–H

Natural Minor Scale:
W–H–W–W–H–W–W

Harmonic Minor Scale:
W–H–W–W–H–WH–H

Melodic Minor Scale:
W–H–W–W–W–W–H

Major Pentatonic Scale:
1–2–3–5–6 (Derived from the major scale)

Minor Pentatonic Scale:
1–b3–4–5–b7 (Derived from the natural minor scale)

Blues Scale:
1–b3–4–b5–5–b7 (Combines elements of the minor pentatonic scale with a blues note)
Dorian Mode:

W–H–W–W–W–H–W

Phrygian Mode:
H–W–W–W–H–W–W

Lydian Mode:
W–W–W–H–W–W–H

Mixolydian Mode:
W–W–H–W–W–H–W

Locrian Mode:
H–W–W–H–W–W–W

Whole Tone Scale:
W–W–W–W–W–W (All whole steps)

Diminished Scale (Half-Whole):
H–W–H–W–H–W–H–W (Repeated pattern of half and whole steps)

Augmented Scale:
W–H–W–H–W–H–W–H (Alternating whole and half steps)

Pentatonic Blues Scale:
1-b3-4-b5-5-b7 (Similar to the minor pentatonic with an added blues note)

These scales serve as the foundation for creating melodies, harmonies, and improvisations in guitar compositions. Experiment with them in different musical contexts to explore their unique sounds and moods.

Additionally, combining scales or adding chromatic notes can further expand your creative palette.

CHORD TONES AND PASSING NOTES

Base your melodic motifs on chord tones to create a strong connection with the underlying harmony. Experiment with passing notes for added interest and tension.

Utilizing chord tones and passing notes is a fundamental aspect of creating engaging and expressive guitar compositions. Chord tones are the notes that belong to a specific chord, while passing notes are non-chord tones that connect chord tones, adding melodic interest.

CHORD TONES

Chord tones are the foundation of a chord and are considered stable, providing a sense of resolution and harmony.

Read on to learn how you can leverage chord tones in your compositions.

Emphasize Chord Changes:
Highlight chord changes by emphasizing the chord tones of each new harmony. This creates a clear and structured musical progression.

Arpeggiate Chords:
Break down chords into individual notes and arpeggiate them. Experiment with different arpeggio patterns to add movement and interest.

Melodic Phrasing:

Build melodic phrases around chord tones. Start or end phrases on chord tones to create a strong sense of resolution.

Voice Leading:

Pay attention to smooth voice leading by connecting chord tones between successive chords. This contributes to a seamless and connected musical flow.

Explore Inversions:

Experiment with chord inversions to vary the arrangement of chord tones. Inverted chords offer new melodic possibilities while maintaining harmonic consistency.

PASSING NOTES

Passing notes connect chord tones and add color, tension, and movement to your compositions.

Let's learn how to effectively incorporate passing notes.

Chromatic Passing Notes:

Introduce chromatic passing notes between chord tones to create tension and release. These non-chord tones can add a touch of dissonance before resolving to a stable chord tone.

Scale-Based Passing Notes:

Use passing notes from the surrounding scale to smoothly connect chord tones. This creates a sense of continuity and can be particularly effective in melodic lines.

Directional Passing Notes:

Experiment with passing notes that lead the melody in a specific direction. This can add a sense of forward motion and guide the listener's ear.

Syncopated Passages:

Insert passing notes in syncopated rhythms to create rhythmic interest. Syncopation can add a dynamic and lively feel to your compositions.

Pedal Tones:

Maintain a repeating bass note (pedal tone) while changing the chords above it. This technique provides stability amidst harmonic movement.

COMBINING CHORD TONES AND PASSING NOTES

Target Chord Tones on Strong Beats:

Align chord tones with strong beats to emphasize harmonic structure. Use passing notes to connect these targeted chord tones.

Create Tension and Release:

Use passing notes strategically to build tension and resolve to stable chord tones. This dynamic interplay enhances the emotional impact of your composition.

Vary Note Durations:

Experiment with different note durations for both chord tones and passing notes. Varying note lengths contributes to the rhythmic complexity of your composition.

Contextual Awareness:

Be mindful of the harmonic context. Consider the chords in the overall progression to choose passing notes that complement the underlying harmony.

By skillfully integrating chord tones and passing notes into your guitar compositions, you can craft melodies that are not only harmonically rich but also melodically compelling. This interplay between stability and tension adds depth and nuance to your musical expression.

ORNAMENTATION TECHNIQUES

Incorporate ornamentation techniques such as slides, hammer-ons, pull-offs, and bends to enhance the character of your melodic phrases.

Ornamentation techniques can add flair, expressiveness, and sophistication to your guitar compositions.

INCORPORATING ORNAMENTATION TECHNIQUES

Slides:

Slide from one note to another, creating a smooth and connected effect. Experiment with different slide lengths and directions for variation.

Hammer-ons and Pull-offs:

Use hammer-ons to produce a legato effect by striking a note and then sounding the next note by tapping a finger onto the fretboard. Pull-offs involve pulling a finger off a fret to sound a lower note.

Trills:

Rapidly alternate between two adjacent notes to create a trill. Trills add a touch of vibrancy and energy to your melodies.

Bends:

Bend a string to raise the pitch of a note. Bends can be subtle or dramatic, and they contribute to the expressive quality of your playing.

Vibrato:

Apply controlled oscillations to a sustained note using the fretting hand. Vibrato adds warmth and expressiveness to the sustained tones in your composition.

Tremolo:

Rapidly repeat a single note or a series of notes to create a tremolo effect. Tremolo can add intensity and energy to your compositions.

Harmonics:

Use natural or artificial harmonics to produce ethereal, bell-like tones. Harmonics can be applied at specific frets or nodes on the string.

Double Stops:

Play two notes simultaneously, often on adjacent strings. Double stops create harmony and can be used for embellishment in melodic lines.

Ghost Notes:

Play muted or lightly fretted notes for a percussive effect. Ghost notes add rhythmic interest and can be effective in funk, blues, or percussive acoustic styles.

Rasgueado:

Employ a flamenco strumming technique involving rapid and consecutive strums with the fingers. Rasgueado adds a fiery and rhythmic character to your compositions.

Glissando:

Slide rapidly between two notes, covering all the pitches in between. Glissandos can be applied across a single string or multiple strings.

String Bending and Release:

Bend a string to raise the pitch and then release it back to its original position. This technique can add expressiveness and drama to your playing.

Palm Muting:

Use the palm of your picking hand to lightly touch the strings near the bridge, creating a muted and percussive effect. Palm muting is often used in rhythmic playing.

Flamenco Techniques (e.g., Picado, Alzapúa):

Explore traditional flamenco techniques such as picado (alternate picking with the fingers) and alzapúa (thumb technique). These techniques are characteristic of flamenco guitar playing.

Bendir Flick:

Mimic the sound of a bendir (a North African frame drum) by flicking the strings with your fingers. This technique adds a percussive and exotic quality.

Experiment with these ornamentation techniques to enhance the expressiveness, dynamics, and overall musicality of your guitar compositions. Combine multiple techniques within your compositions to create a rich and varied sonic palette.

CALL AND RESPONSE PATTERNS

Develop call-and-response patterns within your melody. Play a motif and respond to it with a contrasting or complementary phrase.

Developing call-and-response patterns within your melody is a powerful way to create dynamic, engaging, and conversational musical phrases. The call-and-response technique involves one musical idea (the "call") followed by a contrasting or responsive idea (the "response").

DEVELOPING CALL AND RESPONSE PATTERNS

Identify the Musical Elements:

Start by identifying the key musical elements in your melody that can serve as a call. This could be a specific phrase, motif, or a set of notes. Consider the rhythmic and melodic characteristics that define this initial idea.

Create Contrast for the Response:

The response should offer a contrast to the call, either in terms of melody, rhythm, or both. Introduce new elements that complement or provide a counterpoint to the initial idea. This creates interest and keeps the listener engaged.

Experiment with Rhythmic Variation:

Rhythmic variation is a powerful tool for creating effective call-and-response patterns. If your call features a set rhythm, try altering the rhythmic structure in the response. Syncopation, different note durations, or changing the accent pattern can add excitement.

Explore Melodic Variation:

Vary the melodic content between the call and response. This can involve changing the contour of the melody, introducing new intervals, or altering the overall pitch structure. The goal is to maintain a connection while offering something fresh.

Maintain Consistency in Theme:

While introducing contrast, ensure there is a consistent thematic thread running through both the call and response. This could be a recurring melodic motif, a common rhythmic element, or a shared harmonic progression. Consistency helps tie the phrases together.

Consider Dynamics and Articulation:

Dynamically shaping the call and response adds another layer of expressiveness. Experiment with changes in volume, articulation (e.g., staccato vs. legato), and playing techniques. These variations contribute to the overall dynamic and emotional impact.

THINKING ABOUT QUESTION AND ANSWER

Conceptualize the call as a musical question and the response as an answer. This approach can guide your melodic choices and create a sense of musical dialogue. Craft your phrases to evoke curiosity, tension, and resolution.

Experiment with Different Scales and Modes:

Changing the scale or mode between the call and response can be an effective way to introduce contrast. For example, if the call is in a major key, you might respond with a section in a relative minor key.

Use Repetition Wisely:

Strategic repetition of certain elements can reinforce the call-and-response structure. Repeating a rhythmic motif or melodic fragment in both sections can create a sense of continuity while allowing for variation in other aspects.

Consider Harmonic Progression:

If your composition involves harmonic changes, coordinate the call-and-response structure with these shifts. The response can harmonically complement or contrast with the call, contributing to the overall harmonic development of the piece.

Explore Different Registers:

Utilize different registers of the guitar for the call and response sections. Playing higher on the fretboard for one section and lower for the other, for instance, adds spatial and tonal variety.

Practice and Refine:

Practice the call-and-response sections separately and then together. Refine the timing, phrasing, and dynamics to ensure a seamless and engaging interaction between the call and response. This process may involve iterative refinement.

By integrating call-and-response patterns into your melody, you create a musical conversation that captivates the listener's attention and provides a sense of development and progression within your composition. Experiment with these principles, and let your creativity guide the evolving dialogue between the call and response in your guitar compositions.

CONSIDER SEQUENCING

Use sequencing to repeat and modify melodic patterns. This technique can create a sense of development and continuity in your composition.

UTILIZING SEQUENCING IN COMPOSITION

Sequencing is a technique in music composition where a musical idea, such as a melody or a chord progression, is repeated and transposed to create a pattern or sequence. This method is employed to add structure, cohesion, and interest to a piece of music.

Identify a Motif or Phrase:

Start by identifying a short musical motif, whether it's a melody, chord progression, or even a rhythmic pattern. This will serve as the foundation for your sequence.

Choose a Repetition Pattern:

Decide how you want to repeat the motif. You can repeat it verbatim, or you can modify certain elements, such as rhythm, dynamics, or articulation, with each repetition.

Transposition:

Determine the interval by which you'll transpose the motif for each repetition. Transposing involves shifting the entire motif up or down by a specific pitch interval. This can create a sense of movement and development.

Experiment with Rhythmic Variation:

Varying the rhythm during each repetition can add interest to the sequence. You can experiment with different rhythmic subdivisions, syncopation, or changing the overall rhythmic feel.

Explore Dynamic Changes:

Dynamically shaping each repetition can contribute to the overall expressiveness of the sequence. You might start softly and gradually increase the volume, or vice versa.

Consider Articulation and Techniques:

Experiment with different articulations and playing techniques. For example, you can use legato in one repetition and staccato in the next. This adds texture and variety to the sequence.

Combine Sequencing with Harmony:

If your motif involves harmonic elements, consider how the harmonic progression interacts with the sequencing. You can create harmonic variations alongside the transpositions for added complexity.

Experiment with Different Scales and Modes:

Changing the scale or mode during the sequence can bring a fresh perspective. This is particularly effective if your motif is harmonically rich, as it introduces new tonal colors.

Create Ascending or Descending Patterns:

Decide if you want your sequence to ascend, descend, or follow a specific pattern. Ascending sequences often create a sense of rising tension, while descending sequences may evoke resolution.

Combine Sequencing with Other Techniques:

Integrate sequencing with other compositional techniques, such as modulation, arpeggiation, or chord inversions. This can enhance the complexity and depth of your composition.

Maintain Cohesion:

While sequencing involves repetition and variation, strive to maintain an overall sense of cohesion. The listener should recognize a connection between the different elements of the sequence.

Experiment with Time Signatures:

Changing the time signature during the sequence can introduce rhythmic variety. This is especially effective if your composition allows for unconventional or mixed meter signatures.

Consider the Overall Structure:

Think about the role of sequencing in the overall structure of your composition. It can be used as a building block for larger sections or as a transitional element between different parts of the piece.

Practice and Refine:

Practice playing and listening to the sequenced sections. Refine the timing, dynamics, and any other expressive elements to ensure a polished and well-executed sequence.

Sequencing is a versatile tool that can be applied to various musical elements within your guitar compositions. Whether applied to melodies, chord progressions, or rhythmic patterns, this technique can add depth and sophistication to your music. Experiment with different approaches, and let your creativity guide the development of sequences within your guitar compositions.

ARTICULATION

Experiment with articulation techniques such as legato, staccato, and accents. Articulation choices contribute to the overall character of your melody.

PLAYING WITH ARTICULATION

Articulation is a crucial element in guitar playing and composition. It refers to the way musical notes are performed and how they are connected or separated. By manipulating articulation, you can add expressiveness, dynamics, and nuance to your compositions.

Understand Articulation Techniques:

Familiarize yourself with common articulation techniques such as legato (smooth and connected), staccato (short and detached), hammer-ons, pull-offs, slides, bends, and vibrato. Each technique contributes to the overall character of your composition.

Use Legato for Fluidity:

Legato involves playing notes in a smooth, connected manner. Utilize legato techniques like hammer-ons and pull-offs to create fluid lines. This is effective for conveying a sense of continuity and grace in your melodies.

Incorporate Staccato for Emphasis:

Staccato involves playing notes with a short and detached sound. Integrate staccato to emphasize specific notes or create rhythmic interest. This technique is valuable for adding definition and percussive elements to your composition.

Experiment with Hammer-ons and Pull-offs:

Hammer-ons and pull-offs are techniques where you use the strength of your fretting hand to produce additional notes without picking. Experiment with these techniques to create legato passages or add ornamentation to your melodies.

Explore Slides for Smooth Transitions:

Slides involve smoothly transitioning from one note to another by sliding your finger along the fretboard. Use slides to connect notes and create seamless transitions between different parts of your composition.

Incorporate Bends for Expressiveness:

Bending a string alters the pitch of the note, adding expressiveness to your playing. Experiment with whole-tone bends, half-tone bends, and release bends to infuse emotion into your melodies. Bends are particularly effective for blues and rock genres.

Apply Vibrato for Warmth:

Vibrato is a subtle pitch modulation that adds warmth and expression to sustained notes. Practice different vibrato styles, such as classical, blues, or rock vibrato, and use them strategically to enhance the emotional impact of your composition.

Combine Articulation Techniques:

Don't limit yourself to one articulation technique. Combine techniques within phrases to create diversity and interest. For example, you can start a phrase with a staccato feel and then transition into a legato section for contrast.

Consider the Genre and Mood:

The choice of articulation should align with the genre and mood of your composition. Different styles may have specific articulation preferences, so consider how your choices contribute to the overall feel of the piece.

Pay Attention to Dynamics:

Dynamics play a crucial role in articulation. Experiment with playing softer or louder and consider how it complements your chosen articulation techniques. Dynamic contrast adds depth and intensity to your composition.

Use Articulation for Phrasing:

Think of articulation as a tool for phrasing. Experiment with different articulation patterns to shape the musical phrases in your composition. This helps convey musical ideas more clearly and expressively.

Practice Control and Precision:

Achieving mastery over articulation requires control and precision. Practice each technique slowly and gradually increase the tempo. Focus on producing clean and well-defined articulations.

Record and Analyze:

Record your compositions and listen critically to the articulation. Pay attention to nuances, and consider how different articulation choices impact the overall feel of the piece. Use recording as a tool for refinement.

Seek Inspiration from Other Guitarists:

Listen to and study the playing styles of accomplished guitarists in various genres. Take note of how they use articulation to convey emotion and add character to their compositions.

Experiment with Unconventional Articulations:

Don't be afraid to experiment with unconventional articulations. Create your own techniques or adapt existing ones to suit your unique style. This can lead to innovative and distinctive sounds in your compositions.

Articulation is a powerful tool for enhancing the expressiveness and personality of your guitar compositions. By consciously incorporating different techniques and experimenting with their combinations, you can create music that is dynamic, engaging, and reflective of your artistic vision.

MELODIC REPETITION

Introduce repetition in your melodic motifs. Repeating certain phrases can strengthen the listener's connection to the melody.

INTRODUCING MELODIC REPETITION

Incorporating melodic repetition is a fundamental aspect of crafting memorable and cohesive guitar compositions. Repetition adds structure, familiarity, and catchiness to your melodies, making them more accessible and enjoyable for listeners. Below are some ideas for introducing melodic repetition into your guitar composition.

Establish a Core Melodic Idea:
Begin by creating a core melodic idea that encapsulates the essence of your composition. This could be a distinctive motif, phrase, or sequence of notes that serves as the foundation for the entire piece.

Identify Repetition Points:
Determine strategic points within your composition where repetition can be employed. These can include the opening motif, chorus, bridge, or any section where emphasizing a particular melodic idea enhances the overall impact.

Use Repetition for Emphasis:

Repetition can be used to highlight and emphasize key moments in your composition. Repeating a melodic phrase or motif draws attention to its significance, creating a sense of cohesion and reinforcing the emotional impact.

Experiment with Varied Repetition:

While repetition is a powerful tool, it's essential to balance it with variation to maintain interest. Experiment with varied repetition by introducing subtle changes to the repeated melodic elements. This could involve altering the rhythm, dynamics, or adding ornamentation.

Create Structural Integrity:

Repetition contributes to the structural integrity of your composition. It helps define sections such as verses, choruses, and bridges, providing a sense of organization. Consistent repetition at specific structural points creates a framework that listeners can follow.

Build Anticipation and Recognition:

Repetition builds anticipation and recognition. When listeners encounter a familiar melodic motif, it creates a sense of comfort and engagement. Incorporating repetition strategically ensures that certain musical elements become memorable and recognizable.

Enhance Catchiness and Accessibility:

Catchy and accessible melodies often involve repetition. By crafting melodic ideas that are easy to grasp and repeating them at key junctures, you enhance the overall catchiness of your composition. This is especially important for creating music that resonates with a broad audience.

Consider Lyrics and Vocal Phrasing:

If your composition includes vocals, align the melodic repetition with the phrasing of the lyrics. Repetition can reinforce lyrical themes and make the overall musical experience more cohesive.

Experiment with Repetitive Patterns:

Explore different repetitive patterns within your composition. This could involve repeating a melodic phrase consecutively, creating a call-and-response structure, or employing sequential repetition. Experimenting with patterns adds variety while maintaining the benefits of repetition.

Use Repetition for Development:

Repetition doesn't have to be static. Use it as a tool for development by gradually evolving the repeated elements over time. This could involve subtle changes in instrumentation, dynamics, or harmonization, providing a sense of progression.

Create Contrast through Non-Repetition:

Introduce non-repetitive elements to create contrast. While repetition is valuable, moments of departure from repeated motifs can add intrigue and prevent monotony. Use these contrasting sections strategically to keep your composition dynamic.

Experiment with Different Sections:

Repetition can be applied differently in various sections of your composition. For example, you might use more extensive repetition in the chorus for sing-along appeal, while introducing subtle repetition in verses for thematic continuity.

Balance Predictability and Surprise:

Strike a balance between predictability and surprise. While repetition provides a sense of predictability, occasional surprises or deviations from expected repetitions can add excitement and maintain listener interest.

Record and Evaluate:

Record your composition and listen critically to the repeated sections. Evaluate how repetition contributes to the overall flow and impact. Adjust as needed to achieve the desired balance and effectiveness.

Seek Inspiration from Diverse Genres:

Explore how melodic repetition is utilized in different genres. Listen to a variety of music and analyze how artists across genres employ repetition to create memorable compositions. Adapt and integrate these insights into your own work.

Incorporating melodic repetition requires thoughtful consideration and experimentation. By strategically applying repetition and exploring variations, you can enhance the structure, catchiness, and overall impact of your guitar compositions.

PHRASING

INTRODUCING MELODIC PHRASING

Incorporating phrasing into your guitar composition adds dynamism and interest. We explore phrasing, specific to melodic development below.

Define Musical Phrases:

Start by understanding what constitutes a musical phrase. A phrase is a complete musical thought or idea that often ends with a cadence, creating a sense of closure or pause. Phrases are the building blocks of melodies.

Explore Various Lengths:

Experiment with different phrase lengths within your composition. Short phrases can create a sense of urgency or playfulness, while longer phrases contribute to a more lyrical and flowing quality. Varying phrase lengths adds diversity to your melody.

Align Phrases with Lyricism:

If your composition includes lyrics, align the lengths of your phrases with the natural phrasing of the lyrics. This helps create a seamless integration between the vocal and instrumental elements, enhancing the overall musical experience.

Consider Breath and Pacing:

Imagine phrases as musical sentences, and consider the natural breath and pacing of your composition. Shorter phrases may evoke a quick, breathless quality, while longer phrases provide room for contemplation and expression.

Utilize Antecedent and Consequent Phrases:

Employ the concept of antecedent and consequent phrases. An antecedent phrase sets up an expectation, and the consequent phrase provides a resolution or answer. This creates a sense of musical conversation and keeps the listener engaged.

Build Tension with Longer Phrases:

Longer phrases can be used to build tension and anticipation. Extend the length of a phrase gradually, leading the listener toward a climactic point in your composition. This is effective in creating dynamic and expressive moments.

Create Contrast with Short Phrases:

Introduce contrast by incorporating shorter phrases. Short, punchy phrases can add a sense of rhythmic drive and energy to your composition. Consider using them in more upbeat or rhythmic sections.

Explore Uneven Phrase Lengths:

Break away from uniformity by experimenting with uneven phrase lengths. A combination of short and long phrases can create a sense of unpredictability and keep the listener intrigued.

Align Phrases with Harmonic Changes:

Consider aligning the endings of phrases with harmonic changes. Resolving a phrase at a point of harmonic stability enhances the sense of closure and contributes to the overall harmonic structure of your composition.

Experiment with Repetitive Patterns:

Use repetitive patterns with varying phrase lengths to create interest. Repetition can occur in shorter segments within a longer phrase or in sequences of phrases. This adds a rhythmic and melodic anchor to your composition.

Consider the Overall Arc:

Think about the overall arc of your composition. Arrange phrases to create a sense of development, with shorter phrases introducing ideas and longer phrases expanding on or concluding them. This helps in shaping the narrative of your melody.

Reflect Emotion Through Phrasing:

Tailor the length of phrases to reflect the emotional content of your composition. Longer, more sustained phrases may convey introspection or melancholy, while shorter, staccato phrases can evoke excitement or tension.

Use Rests for Emphasis:

Introduce rests strategically within and between phrases. A well-placed rest can create emphasis, punctuate a musical idea, and contribute to the overall rhythmic feel of your composition.

Record and Evaluate:

Record your melody and listen critically to the interplay of different phrase lengths. Assess how the phrases contribute to the overall character and mood of your composition. Make adjustments as needed for optimal flow.

Draw Inspiration from Different Genres:

Explore how phrase lengths are utilized in various musical genres. Analyze compositions from different styles to gain insights into the effective use of phrase lengths. Adapt and incorporate these techniques into your own guitar compositions.

By carefully considering and manipulating phrase lengths, you can enhance the expressiveness, narrative, and rhythmic interest of your guitar melodies. Experiment with different approaches, and let the unique qualities of your composition guide your decisions regarding phrase lengths.

MELODIC RECORDING

Record your melodic ideas and listen critically. Pay attention to how they fit into the overall composition and make adjustments as needed.

RECORD AND LISTEN

Recording and critically listening to your melodies is a valuable practice for refining your guitar compositions. Let's explore the recording process in more depth so you can review and bring out the best in your melodies.

Use Quality Recording Equipment:
Invest in a good-quality microphone and recording interface to capture the nuances of your guitar playing accurately. This ensures that your recordings reflect the true character of your melodies.

Consider Room Acoustics:
Pay attention to the acoustics of the recording space. Minimize background noise and choose a room with favorable acoustics to enhance the clarity of your guitar melodies.

Experiment with Microphone Placement:
Test different microphone placements to find the position that captures the best sound. Experiment with close miking, room miking, and various angles to achieve the desired tonal characteristics.

Ensure Proper Levels:

Set appropriate recording levels to avoid distortion or clipping. Aim for a clean and balanced recording that accurately represents the dynamics of your playing.

Record in High Quality:

Opt for high-resolution recording formats (e.g., 24-bit/96kHz) to capture the full range of frequencies and subtle details in your guitar melodies.

Consider Multiple Takes:

Record multiple takes of your melodies. This allows you to choose the best performance and provides flexibility during the editing process.

Record Different Articulations:

Experiment with various playing techniques and articulations. Record passages with different dynamics, picking styles, and nuances to explore the expressive possibilities of your melodies.

Use High-Quality Playback Systems:

When evaluating your recordings, use high-quality headphones or speakers to ensure an accurate representation of the sound. Avoid using devices with limited frequency response.

Listen for Clarity and Articulation:

Pay attention to the clarity and articulation of each note. Ensure that individual notes are distinct and that the overall performance captures the intended expressiveness.

Assess Dynamics and Phrasing:

Evaluate the dynamic range of your performance. Check for effective use of dynamics, such as crescendos and decrescendos, and assess how well the phrasing conveys the intended emotions.

Check Timing and Rhythm:

Examine the timing and rhythm of your melodies. Ensure that your playing is in time and that rhythmic elements contribute to the overall groove and feel of the composition.

Evaluate Tone and Timbre:

Analyze the tone and timbre of your guitar. Ensure that the chosen tonal qualities align with the mood and theme of your composition. Make adjustments to the recording or playing technique if needed.

Assess Sustain and Decay:

Consider the sustain and decay of notes. Evaluate how well sustained notes carry, especially in legato passages, and ensure that decay complements the phrasing and pacing of your melodies.

Check for Unwanted Noise:

Listen for any unwanted noise, such as string squeaks, fret buzz, or background interference. Address these issues during the recording process or in post-production.

Evaluate Stereo Imaging (if applicable):

If you recorded in stereo, assess the stereo imaging. Ensure a balanced distribution of sound between the left and right channels, and consider whether the spatial elements enhance the listening experience.

Consider Emotional Impact:

Assess whether your melodies evoke the intended emotions. Consider how the interplay of musical elements contributes to the overall mood and theme of your composition.

Take Notes for Improvement:

Make detailed notes on areas that need improvement or adjustment. This could include specific passages, tonal qualities, or expressive elements that can be refined for a more polished result.

Compare Different Takes:

If you recorded multiple takes, compare them to identify the strengths of each. Choose the take that best aligns with your artistic vision and the goals of your composition.

Seek External Feedback:

Share your recordings with trusted peers, mentors, or collaborators for external feedback. Fresh perspectives can provide valuable insights and help you refine your melodies further.

Iterate and Refine:

Based on your evaluations and feedback, make necessary adjustments and re-record if needed. The process of iteration and refinement is crucial for achieving a final recording that aligns with your creative vision.

By approaching the recording and critical listening process with attention to detail and a discerning ear, you can refine your guitar melodies and elevate the overall quality of your compositions. Regularly recording and evaluating your work will contribute to your growth as a guitarist and composer.

REFINE AND SIMPLIFY

Refine your melodic motifs by eliminating any unnecessary complexity. Sometimes, simplicity can enhance the emotional impact of a melody.

STREAMLINING AND IMPROVEMENTS

Refining and simplifying your arrangements in guitar composition can enhance clarity, accessibility, and overall effectiveness.

Identify Core Elements:

Identify the essential elements of your composition. What are the core melodies, harmonies, and rhythms? Focus on preserving these elements while simplifying the surrounding textures.

Streamline Chord Progressions:

Simplify complex chord progressions. Consider using basic triads or open chords to maintain harmonic richness while reducing complexity. Strive for a balance between harmonic interest and accessibility.

Reduce Redundancy:

Eliminate unnecessary repetition or redundancy. Evaluate whether each section of your composition serves a unique purpose. If certain elements are repetitive without adding significant value, consider simplifying or omitting them.

Clarify Melodic Lines:

Ensure that your melodic lines are clear and memorable. Simplify intricate melodies by focusing on key motifs or phrases. Emphasize simplicity in the main themes to enhance their impact.

Limit the Number of Voices:

Reduce the number of simultaneous voices in your arrangements. For solo guitar compositions, especially, limiting the number of voices can enhance clarity. Prioritize the primary melody and supporting harmonies.

Simplify Fingerpicking Patterns:

If your composition involves fingerstyle guitar, simplify intricate fingerpicking patterns. Focus on maintaining a steady rhythm and emphasize key notes. This makes the piece more accessible to a wider audience.

Optimize Instrumentation:

If your composition includes multiple instruments, optimize the instrumentation. Assign distinct roles to each instrument, avoiding unnecessary overlap. This ensures a clear and balanced sound.

Reduce Ornamentation:

Minimize ornamental elements, especially if they contribute to unnecessary complexity. While ornamentation can add flair, excessive embellishments might distract from the core musical ideas.

Evaluate Dynamics:

Evaluate the dynamic range of your composition. While dynamics are crucial for expressiveness, consider simplifying dynamic changes to create a more straightforward listening experience.

Focus on Transitions:

Pay attention to transitions between sections. Smooth transitions contribute to the overall flow of your composition. Simplify transitions by maintaining consistent elements or using simple connecting phrases.

Use Pacing Effectively:

Manage the pacing of your composition. Allow moments of rest and simplicity to contrast with more intricate sections. This provides a dynamic listening experience and prevents overwhelming complexity.

Test with Others:

Play your simplified arrangements for others and gather feedback. Observing how listeners respond can help you identify areas that may still need refinement or simplification.

Iterative Refinement:

Refine your arrangement iteratively. Make adjustments based on feedback and your own critical evaluation. Simplification is often a gradual process that improves over time.

Record and Analyze:

Record your simplified arrangements and critically listen. Pay attention to how the simplified elements contribute to the overall impact of the composition. Use recordings to identify areas for further improvement.

Embrace Silence:

Don't underestimate the power of silence. Strategic use of pauses and breaks can enhance the impact of your composition. Allow moments of simplicity to stand out against a backdrop of silence.

Remember, simplifying doesn't mean sacrificing creativity or expression. It's about distilling your musical ideas to their essence and creating a more accessible and engaging experience for your audience.

DISTILL THE MELODY

Distilling the musical essence in a melody for guitar composition involves refining and focusing on the core elements that capture the emotion, theme, and character you intend to convey.

DISTILLING MUSICAL ESSENCE

Identify Core Themes:

Clarify the central themes or emotions you want to express through your melody. Whether it's joy, melancholy, or excitement, having a clear understanding of your musical intentions is crucial.

Simplify Melodic Ideas:

Streamline your initial melodic ideas. Remove any unnecessary embellishments or complexities. Aim for simplicity while retaining the essence of your intended mood or theme.

Focus on Key Motifs:

Identify key motifs or recurring musical phrases within your melody. These motifs act as anchors, providing a cohesive structure and making it easier for listeners to connect with your composition.

Embrace Silence:

Integrate moments of silence strategically. Silence is a powerful tool that can enhance the impact of your melody. Allow space for the music to breathe, creating a dynamic and engaging listening experience.

Highlight Key Notes:

Emphasize certain notes within your melody that carry the most emotional weight. These key notes contribute to the overall mood and can serve as focal points that resonate with listeners.

Experiment with Dynamics:

Use dynamic contrasts to highlight the expressive elements of your melody. Experiment with variations in volume, emphasizing certain phrases or creating subtle nuances to evoke specific emotions.

Consider Articulation:

Pay attention to articulation, including legato, staccato, and accents. Each articulation choice influences the character of your melody. Choose articulations that align with the emotional essence you're aiming for.

Clarify Harmonic Support:

Ensure that the harmonic support complements and enhances the essence of your melody. Simplify chord progressions or harmonies to create a supportive backdrop without overshadowing the melodic core.

Capture Emotional Resonance:

Evaluate how well your melody captures the emotional resonance you seek. The musical essence should evoke a genuine emotional response, connecting with both the performer and the listener on a deeper level.

Connect with Theme or Story:

If your melody is part of a larger composition with a theme or story, ensure that it aligns seamlessly with these elements. The melody should be a narrative thread that enhances the overall storytelling.

Refine Rhythmic Elements:

Refine the rhythmic elements of your melody. Ensure that the rhythm supports the emotional tone and provides a rhythmic foundation that is both engaging and cohesive.

Evaluate Melodic Contour:

Assess the overall contour of your melody. Consider the rise and fall of pitches and how they contribute to the emotional journey. Aim for a contour that reflects the intended mood and energy.

Eliminate Redundancy:

Remove any redundant or repetitive elements that do not contribute significantly to the musical essence. Every note and phrase should serve a purpose in conveying the intended emotion or theme.

Experiment with Instrumentation:

If applicable, experiment with different guitar techniques or instrumentation to enhance the essence of your melody. Consider the timbre and textures that best express your musical vision.

Capture Authenticity:

Infuse your melody with authenticity and personal expression. The most powerful melodies often resonate deeply when they reflect the genuine emotions and experiences of the composer.

Continuous Iteration:

Engage in continuous iteration. Revisit and refine your melody over time. As you gain new perspectives, you may discover ways to further distill and enhance the musical essence.

Remember that distilling the musical essence is an ongoing process that involves both intuition and thoughtful analysis. Trust your instincts, stay connected to your creative vision, and refine your melody until it becomes a distilled, powerful expression of your musical intent.

Creating melodies is a deeply personal process, and there are no strict rules. Trust your instincts, be open to exploration, and let the essence of your composition guide the development of captivating melodic motifs on the guitar.

TUNINGS

Exploring different tunings and techniques on the guitar is a fantastic way to unlock unique sounds and textures in your compositions.

EXPLORATION OF TUNINGS AND TECHNIQUES

Exploring different tunings and techniques in guitar composition opens up a world of creative possibilities and allows you to achieve unique sounds that may not be possible with standard approaches.

There are many compelling reasons why you should explore different tunings and techniques for your guitar compositions.

Unique Sonic Palette:

Different tunings offer distinct sonic landscapes. Experimenting with alternative tunings expands your sonic palette, enabling you to create textures and tonalities that are not achievable in standard tuning. This uniqueness can make your compositions stand out and be more memorable.

Expressive Possibilities:

Various techniques, such as alternate picking, fingerstyle, tapping, and slides, provide different ways to express emotions and convey musical ideas. Exploring these techniques allows you to infuse your compositions with a wide range of expressive possibilities, adding depth and nuance to your music.

Innovation and Creativity:

Embracing unconventional tunings and techniques encourages innovation and creativity. It challenges you to think outside the conventional musical norms and discover new ways to approach composition. This experimentation can lead to groundbreaking ideas and a distinctive musical voice.

Personalized Style:

Developing your unique guitar style involves exploring different tunings and techniques. As you discover what resonates with you, you can incorporate these elements into your compositions, contributing to the development of a personalized and recognizable musical identity.

Enhanced Emotional Expression:

Certain tunings and techniques can evoke specific emotions or moods. By tailoring your guitar composition to unique tunings or playing techniques, you can enhance the emotional expression of your music, making it more poignant and resonant with listeners.

Adaptation to Themes or Concepts:

If your composition is inspired by a particular theme or concept, experimenting with tunings and techniques can help you sonically represent that theme. For example, if your composition is nature-inspired, exploring tunings that mimic natural sounds can enhance the thematic connection.

Textural Variety:

Different tunings and techniques introduce textural variety into your compositions. This diversity can be especially beneficial in creating dynamic contrasts within a piece, keeping the listener engaged and interested in the unfolding musical narrative.

Expanded Range and Harmonic Options:

Alternative tunings may provide an expanded range of pitches and harmonic possibilities. This can be advantageous in crafting intricate chord voicings, harmonies, and melodic lines that may be challenging or impossible in standard tuning.

Genre Fusion:

If you're interested in genre fusion, experimenting with different tunings and techniques allows you to blend elements from various musical styles. This fusion can result in a hybrid sound that is fresh, innovative, and appeals to a broader audience.

Overcoming Creative Blocks:

When facing creative blocks or feeling uninspired, trying out new tunings or techniques can reignite your creative spark. It introduces an element of surprise and discovery, helping you break away from familiar patterns and generate new musical ideas.

Enhanced Fingerstyle Possibilities:

For fingerstyle guitarists, exploring alternate tunings opens up a world of possibilities for fingerpicking patterns, harmonics, and intricate fretting techniques.

This can significantly enrich the texture and complexity of your compositions.

Aesthetic Variety in Composition:

Incorporating different tunings and techniques adds aesthetic variety to your compositions. This variety keeps your music interesting and can lead to a more engaging listening experience for your audience.

Remember that while exploring different tunings and techniques is valuable, it's equally important to maintain a balance and ensure that these choices serve the overall musicality and intention of your composition. Strive for a harmonious integration of these elements, allowing your creativity to flourish and your guitar compositions to reach new heights.

TUNING EXPERIMENTATION

Experimentation with different tunings will add distinctiveness to your guitar composition. Let's do some experiments through exploration of different tuning variations.

Standard Tuning Variations:

Experiment with alternative tunings within the standard tuning framework.

For example, drop D tuning (D–A–D–G–B–E) or open G tuning (D–G–D–G–B–D) can provide different harmonic possibilities.

Alternative tunings within the standard tuning framework provide guitarists with an opportunity to explore fresh sonic landscapes without deviating significantly from the familiar six-string setup. These alternative tunings involve adjusting the pitches of individual strings while retaining the relative intervals between them.

Alternative tunings within Standard Tuning Framework

Drop D Tuning (D A D G B E):

Drop D is a popular alternative tuning where the sixth string is tuned down a whole step to D. This tuning enhances power chords and allows for a deep, resonant low D note. It's widely used in rock, metal, and folk genres, providing a heavier and fuller sound.

Open D Tuning (D A D F# A D):

Open D tuning creates a D major chord when strummed open. It is well-suited for slide guitar and fingerstyle playing. The tuning facilitates the creation of rich, open chords and encourages exploration of harmonics, making it a favorite for blues and folk musicians.

Open G Tuning (D G D G B D):

Open G tuning, popularized by Keith Richards of The Rolling Stones, creates a G major chord when strummed open. It's versatile for slide guitar and fingerstyle playing and is commonly used in blues and rock. The open G tuning offers a resonant and vibrant sound.

DADGAD Tuning (D A D G A D):

DADGAD is a modal tuning that provides a drone-like quality. It's commonly used in folk, Celtic, and acoustic fingerstyle genres. The open strings create a Dsus4 chord, and this tuning encourages experimentation with unique chord voicings and melodic possibilities.

Double Drop D Tuning (D A D G B D):

Double Drop D combines elements of Drop D and Open D tunings. Both the sixth and first strings are tuned down a whole step to D. This tuning is versatile, allowing for power chords on the low D string and open chords on the high strings. It's suitable for various styles, including rock and folk.

Open E Tuning (E B E G# B E):

Open E tuning creates an E major chord when strummed open. It's popular in slide guitar playing and provides a bright, ringing quality. This tuning encourages the exploration of slide techniques and facilitates the creation of major and minor chords with a single finger barring.

Open A Tuning (E A E A C# E):

Open A tuning creates an A major chord when strummed open. It's suitable for both fingerstyle and slide playing. This tuning offers a warm and resonant sound, making it well-suited for blues and folk compositions.

Dropped C Tuning (C G C F A D):

Dropped C tuning involves tuning the sixth string down to C. It's commonly used in metal and alternative rock genres, providing a heavier and lower tonal range. This tuning enhances power chords and facilitates deep, chugging riffs.

Open C Tuning (C G C G C E):

Open C tuning creates a C major chord when strummed open. It's popular for slide guitar playing and has a rich, full sound. This tuning is versatile and can be applied to various genres, including blues and folk.

Half-Step Down Tuning (Eb Ab Db Gb Bb eb):

While not a drastic departure, tuning all strings down by a half step (Eb Ab Db Gb Bb eb) can impart a different tonal character. This tuning is employed by many rock and metal guitarists and can add a slightly lower and darker quality to the sound.

Experimenting with these alternative tunings within the standard tuning framework allows you to discover new chord voicings, melodic possibilities, and tonal textures. As you explore these tunings, consider how they complement the mood and theme of your composition, and embrace the creative freedom they offer in shaping your unique guitar sound.

OPEN TUNINGS

Explore open tunings where the strings are tuned to form a chord. Popular open tunings include open D (D–A–D–F#–A–D) or open E (E–B–E–G#–B–E). These tunings offer unique harmonic palettes.

Open tunings are a fascinating and creative approach for guitar composition, offering unique possibilities for chord voicings, resonant drones, and expressive slide playing. In open tunings, the guitar is tuned to form a chord when strummed open without fretting any notes.

Open D Tuning (D A D F# A D):

Open D tuning creates a D major chord when strummed open. This tuning is well-suited for folk, blues, and slide guitar. It encourages the use of resonant open chords and facilitates slide playing with a bluesy character.

Open G Tuning (D G D G B D):

Open G tuning creates a G major chord when strummed open. Widely used in blues and rock, this tuning provides a vibrant and resonant sound. The open strings create rich, full chords, and slide playing in this tuning is common.

Open E Tuning (E B E G# B E):

Open E tuning creates an E major chord when strummed open. It's popular for slide guitar, offering a bright and ringing quality. This tuning encourages the exploration of slide techniques and allows for expressive single-finger chords.

Open A Tuning (E A C# E A E):

Open A tuning creates an A major chord when strummed open. Suitable for blues and folk, this tuning produces a warm and resonant sound. It's versatile for both fingerstyle and slide guitar playing.

Open C Tuning (C G C G C E):

Open C tuning creates a C major chord when strummed open. Ideal for slide guitar, this tuning has a rich, full sound. It encourages exploration of unique chord voicings and resonant drone notes.

Open G Minor Tuning (D G D G Bb D):

Similar to Open G but with a lowered third, Open G Minor creates a G minor chord when strummed open. It's suitable for creating a melancholic or bluesy atmosphere in your compositions.

DADGAD Tuning (D A D G A D):

DADGAD is a modal tuning with a drone-like quality. Commonly used in folk and acoustic music, it encourages experimentation with chord voicings and unique melodic possibilities.

Open C6 Tuning (C A C G C E):

Open C6 tuning creates a C6 chord when strummed open. It's suitable for jazz and Hawaiian music, providing a bright and jazzy sound. The major sixth interval offers interesting chord voicings.

Open D Minor Tuning (D A D F A D):

Open D Minor tuning creates a D minor chord when strummed open. It's excellent for exploring minor key compositions and can evoke a haunting or mysterious mood.

Open E Minor Tuning (E B E G B E):

Open E Minor tuning creates an E minor chord when strummed open. It's versatile for both major and minor key compositions, offering a darker and expressive tonal palette.

When working with open tunings, consider the mood and theme of your composition. Experiment with the resonant qualities of open strings, explore unique chord voicings, and take advantage of the opportunities for expressive slide playing. Additionally, open tunings can inspire new melodic ideas and provide a fresh perspective on your guitar composition. Embrace the creative freedom that open tunings offer and let them shape the sonic landscape of your music.

DROPPED AND RAISED TUNINGS

Lower or raise specific strings to create dropped or raised tunings. This can result in richer chords and altered tonalities.

Dropped and raised tunings are alternative tuning configurations that can significantly influence the sonic possibilities of your guitar compositions. These tunings involve adjusting the pitch of one or more strings, deviating from the standard EADGBE tuning.

Dropped Tunings:

Drop D Tuning (D A D G B E):

Lowering the low E string to D opens up possibilities for powerful and resonant low-end riffs. Common in rock and metal genres, it provides a heavier sound.

Drop C Tuning (C G C F A D):

Extending the drop concept further, Drop C offers even lower tones, enhancing the dark and aggressive qualities. Popular in metal and alternative rock.

Double Drop D Tuning (D A D G B D):

Similar to Drop D but with both E strings tuned down to D. This tuning is versatile, lending itself to both heavy and melodic playing.

Drop B Tuning (B F# B E G# C#):

Frequently used in extreme metal genres, Drop B provides a deep and intense sound, allowing for intricate riffing and powerful chords.

Raised Tunings:

Raised G Tuning (D G D G B D):

Raising the low E string to G can create an open and bright sound. It's suitable for folk, country, and fingerstyle playing, offering a unique tonal palette.

High Strung or Nashville Tuning (E A D G B E):

Keeping the standard EADGBE tuning for the lower strings and using octave strings for the higher strings results in a bright and jangly sound. Great for adding sparkle to acoustic compositions.

Raised B Tuning (F# B E A C# F#):

Increasing the pitch of the low E string to B can create a unique tonal landscape, suitable for experimental or ambient compositions.

CREATIVE APPLICATIONS FOR DROPPED TUNINGS

Expanded Range:

Dropped tunings provide a lower pitch range, enhancing the guitar's capacity for heavy, aggressive, or intricate playing.

Tonal Variety:

Raised tunings introduce different tonal qualities, offering a fresh perspective on familiar chord shapes and melodic patterns.

Emotional Resonance:

Experimenting with different tunings can evoke specific emotions. For example, dropped tunings might convey power and intensity, while raised tunings could bring out a brighter, more delicate mood.

Instrumental Texture:

Dropped tunings can create a fuller, more resonant sound, especially in solo or instrumental compositions. Raised tunings, on the other hand, can add clarity and sparkle to intricate fingerstyle arrangements.

Genre Exploration:

Different tunings are associated with various genres. Dropped tunings are prevalent in heavy genres like metal, while raised tunings find a place in folk, country, and alternative styles.

As you explore dropped and raised tunings, consider how they complement the themes and emotions you aim to convey in your compositions. Embrace the creative possibilities these tunings offer and let them inspire unique and captivating musical expressions.

MODAL TUNINGS

Experiment with modal tunings, such as DADGAD or CGCGCD. Modal tunings can evoke specific moods and are commonly used in folk and world music.

Modal tunings refer to alternate guitar tunings that emphasize the characteristics of specific musical modes, allowing for distinct harmonic possibilities. Each mode has its unique set of intervals, and tuning the guitar to resonate with these intervals can inspire compositions with modal flavors.

Dorian Tuning (D A D G A D):

Intervals: Whole, Whole, Half, Whole, Whole, Whole, Half

Creative Applications: Dorian mode has a minor tonality with a bright and uplifting quality. This tuning is suitable for creating modal progressions that evoke a sense of adventure or mystery. It's often used in folk, blues, and rock.

Mixolydian Tuning (D G C G C D):

Intervals: Whole, Whole, Half, Whole, Whole, Half, Whole

Creative Applications: Mixolydian mode has a bluesy and dominant sound. This tuning can enhance the characteristic tension of the Mixolydian mode, making it ideal for blues, rock, or fusion compositions.

Lydian Tuning (C G D A E G):

Intervals: Whole, Whole, Whole, Half, Whole, Whole, Half

Creative Applications: Lydian mode has a dreamy and ethereal quality. This tuning emphasizes the Lydian mode's raised fourth, creating a unique and atmospheric tonality. Well-suited for ambient, experimental, or cinematic compositions.

Open D Maj7 Tuning (D A D F# A D):

Intervals: Whole, Whole, Whole, Half, Whole, Whole, Whole

Creative Applications: This tuning emphasizes a major seventh chord, offering a lush and jazzy tonality. Ideal for creating compositions with a sophisticated and harmonically rich sound.

Open G Maj9 Tuning (D G D F# A D):

Intervals: Whole, Whole, Whole, Whole, Whole, Half, Whole

Creative Applications: Featuring a major ninth chord, this tuning provides a bright and expansive quality. It's well-suited for compositions that aim for a cheerful, optimistic, or uplifting atmosphere.

Phrygian Tuning (C G C F Bb C):

Intervals: Half, Whole, Whole, Whole, Half, Whole, Whole

Creative Applications: Phrygian mode has a distinctive Spanish or Middle Eastern sound. This tuning enhances the Phrygian mode's minor tonality and is excellent for compositions with a mysterious or exotic vibe.

TIPS FOR MODAL TUNINGS

Exploration of Modes:

Each modal tuning encourages exploration of the unique characteristics of a particular mode. Experiment with chord progressions and melodic lines that highlight the modal flavor.

Expressive Melodies:

Modal tunings can inspire expressive and emotive melodies that align with the mood of the chosen mode.

Genre Fusion:

Modal tunings can be used to fuse different genres, creating compositions that blend traditional modes with contemporary styles.

Dynamic Playing:

Modal tunings often open up opportunities for dynamic playing, allowing you to emphasize the strengths of each mode through varied techniques and articulations.

Remember, modal tunings offer a distinctive sonic palette, and their creative applications extend beyond traditional tonalities. As you delve into modal tunings, consider the emotional impact of each mode and how it aligns with the themes and atmospheres you want to convey in your guitar compositions.

MICROTONAL TUNINGS

Venture into microtonal tunings where the traditional 12-tone scale is expanded. This opens the door to more intervals and a broader sonic palette.

Microtonal tunings involve dividing the traditional Western musical scale into intervals smaller than the standard half-step, introducing microtones. These tunings provide a unique and experimental approach to guitar composition, allowing for a broader range of pitches and expressive possibilities.

OVERVIEW OF MICROTONAL TUNINGS

Quarter-Tone Tuning:
Intervals: Quarter-tones (half of a standard half-step)

Example Tuning: E A D G B E (with each fret representing a quarter-tone)

Creative Applications: Allows for subtle pitch variations, creating expressive and nuanced melodies. Well-suited for experimental, avant-garde, or world music compositions.

Just Intonation Tuning:

Intervals: Based on simple integer ratios, creating pure harmonic relationships

Example Tuning: Customized based on chosen intervals

Creative Applications: Provides a more natural and consonant sound, enhancing harmonic purity. Suitable for compositions with a focus on rich, resonant chords and intervals.

19-Tone Equal Temperament (19-EDO):

Intervals: Divides the octave into 19 equal parts

Example Tuning: Customized based on the 19-EDO system

Creative Applications: Offers a balance between microtonal exploration and compatibility with Western music. Enables the creation of intricate melodic lines with unique tonalities.

Harry Partch's Just Intonation Guitar:

Intervals: Based on Partch's 43-tone scale

Example Tuning: Customized according to Partch's specifications

Creative Applications: Partch's tuning system opens up a vast array of microtonal possibilities, allowing for compositions with a truly unique and otherworldly sound.

CREATIVE TIPS FOR MICROTONAL TUNINGS

Exploration of New Harmonies: Microtonal tunings provide an opportunity to explore harmonies that go beyond traditional Western tonalities. Experiment with chord progressions and voicings that take advantage of microtonal intervals.

Expressive Bending and Slides:

Utilize microtonal intervals for expressive bending and sliding techniques. This adds a dynamic and emotive quality to your compositions.

Hybrid Tunings:

Combine microtonal strings with standard-tuned strings to create hybrid tunings. This allows for a gradual transition between microtonal and traditional tonalities.

Collaboration with Other Instruments:

Consider collaborating with other musicians who play microtonal instruments. This can lead to innovative and cross-cultural compositions.

Customized Tunings:

Experiment with creating your own microtonal tunings based on specific intervals that resonate with your artistic vision. Customization allows for a personalized approach to microtonal composition.

Remember, microtonal tunings require a willingness to explore and push the boundaries of traditional Western music. Embrace the unconventional nature of microtonality and let it inspire your guitar compositions in ways that traditional tuning systems might not allow.

CUSTOM TUNING CREATION

Design your own custom tuning by adjusting individual strings. This allows for a highly personalized approach tailored to your composition.

Creating your own tunings for guitar composition can be a highly rewarding and personalized approach to shaping your musical sound.

STEPS TO CREATE YOUR OWN GUITAR TUNING

Define Your Objective:

Clarify the musical goals you want to achieve. Are you looking for a specific tonal quality, exploring unique intervals, or aiming for a certain mood? Knowing your objective will guide your tuning choices.

Understand Intervals:

Have a basic understanding of musical intervals. Consider which intervals resonate with your musical vision. Common intervals include major thirds, fifths, and sevenths, but you can also experiment with less conventional intervals.

Experiment with String Tension:

Adjust the tension of each string to achieve the desired feel. Higher tension can provide a tight and responsive feel, while lower tension may offer a more relaxed and expressive touch.

Explore Non-Standard Intervals:

Experiment with intervals that go beyond the standard Western twelve-tone system. This could involve quarter-tones, just intonation ratios, or any custom interval you find musically intriguing.

Consider Symmetry:

Create symmetrical patterns if you want consistency across different strings. Symmetry can make it easier to transpose chords and scales, adding a sense of coherence to your tuning.

Balance Open Strings and Fretted Notes:

Balance the use of open strings and fretted notes. Open strings can provide resonance and unique harmonic possibilities, while fretted notes allow for precise control over pitch.

Think About Chord Voicings:

Consider how your tuning affects chord voicings. Some tunings may naturally lend themselves to certain chord shapes, while others might offer more dissonant or complex voicings.

Experiment Gradually:

Make small adjustments to your tuning and play around with different combinations. Listen carefully to how each change impacts the overall sound and feel of the instrument.

Document Your Tuning:

Once you find a tuning you like, document it for future reference. Write down the pitches of each string or create a diagram. This documentation will be valuable as you work on compositions using the tuning.

Be Open to Revisions:

Don't hesitate to revisit and revise your tuning as you compose. You might discover new possibilities or find that certain adjustments better suit your evolving musical ideas.

EXAMPLE OF CREATING A CUSTOM TUNING

Let's say you want to create a tuning that emphasizes a dreamy and open quality:

Custom Dreamy Tuning:
1st (high E): E
2nd: B
3rd: G
4th: D
5th: A
6th (low E): D

This tuning creates a lush and open sound with intervals that complement each other, encouraging the exploration of ethereal and atmospheric compositions.

Remember, the key is to be curious, playful, and open to the unique possibilities that your custom tuning can unlock in your guitar compositions.

TECHNIQUES

Exploring techniques like capo positioning, fingerstyles and harmonics can kick your guitar composition up several notches, making it unique and setting apart from the pack. Let's dive in.

USE CAPOS CREATIVELY

Combine alternative tunings with capo positions to experiment with different tonalities and voicings. The capo can effectively change the key and alter the mood of your composition.

Using capos creatively in guitar composition is an excellent way to explore new tonal possibilities and expand your musical palette.

UNDERSTANDING THE BASICS

A capo is a device placed across the guitar neck to shorten the vibrating length of the strings. This effectively raises the pitch of the guitar, allowing you to play in different keys without changing the fingerings of chords.

Types of Capos:
There are various types of capos, including spring-loaded, elastic, and partial capos. Each type has its own characteristics, affecting the pressure applied to the strings and the overall sound.

Transposing Keys:
The primary function of a capo is to change the key of a song. Experiment with placing the capo on different

frets to find the tonal range that suits the mood of your composition.

Creating Open Chord Voicings:

Use a capo to create open chord voicings that might be challenging in standard tuning. This can lead to unique and resonant sounds, especially when combined with open strings.

Enhancing Fingerstyle Techniques:

Capos can facilitate intricate fingerstyle techniques by providing a clear and defined sound on open strings. Explore how capos can enhance the expressiveness of your fingerpicking.

Mimicking Alternate Tunings:

Achieve the sound of alternate tunings without retuning your guitar by using a capo in conjunction with standard tuning. This allows you to experiment with different tonal qualities easily.

Layering Sounds:

Combine capoed and non-capoed sections within a composition to create dynamic contrasts. This can add depth and complexity to your music, especially when transitioning between different parts.

Capo as a Creative Tool:

Treat the capo as a creative tool rather than just a practical accessory. Experiment with unconventional capo placements, such as placing it on only a few strings, to produce unique textures.

Partial Capo Techniques:

Explore partial capo techniques, where the capo covers only specific strings. This approach can unlock interesting harmonic possibilities and create a distinctive sound signature.

Capo Combinations:

Combine the use of capos with alternative tunings or alternate chord voicings. This layered approach can lead to rich, complex, and innovative sounds in your compositions.

EXAMPLE OF CREATIVE CAPO USE

Let's say you want to create a bright and jangly sound reminiscent of a ukulele.

Capoed Ukulele-style Tuning:
1st (high E): A (capo on the 5th fret)
2nd: E (capo on the 5th fret)
3rd: C (capo on the 5th fret)
4th: G (capo on the 5th fret)
5th: B (capo on the 5th fret)
6th (low E): E (capo on the 5th fret)
This capo placement mimics the tuning of a ukulele, providing a bright and cheerful tone that can inspire playful and uplifting compositions.

Remember to approach capo usage with curiosity, and don't be afraid to break away from conventional placements. The capo can be a powerful ally in your exploration of unique sounds and creative expression in guitar composition.

FINGERSTYLE TECHNIQUES

Incorporate various fingerstyle techniques such as fingerpicking, Travis picking, and percussive tapping. These techniques add intricate textures to your compositions.

Fingerstyle techniques offer a wide range of expressive possibilities for guitar composition.

Fingerpicking Patterns:

Experiment with various fingerpicking patterns, such as Travis picking, alternating bass notes, or arpeggios. These patterns create a rhythmic and melodic foundation for your composition.

Thumb-Index-Middle Fingerstyle:

Develop independence between your thumb, index, and middle fingers. This classic fingerstyle approach allows you to play bass notes with the thumb while picking melody and harmony with the other fingers.

Classical PIMA Finger Notation:

Use the PIMA notation (Thumb, Index, Middle, Ring, and Pinky) commonly associated with classical guitar. This notation helps organize finger assignments for specific strings and enhances precision.

Fingerstyle Chords:

Explore fingerstyle chord voicings where each finger plays a different note within a chord. This technique adds richness and complexity to your harmonic structures.

Harmonics:

Integrate harmonics by lightly touching the strings at specific nodes while plucking. Natural harmonics and artificial harmonics can create ethereal and bell-like tones.

Percussive Elements:

Incorporate percussive elements by tapping the guitar body or slapping the strings with your palm. This adds rhythmic diversity and percussive accents to your compositions.

Hammer-ons and Pull-offs:

Enhance melodic passages with hammer-ons and pull-offs. These techniques involve playing notes without picking, creating smooth and legato transitions between tones.

Slides and Glissandos:

Use slides to transition smoothly between two notes or create expressive glissandos. Slides add a vocal quality to your playing and can convey emotion effectively.

Fingerstyle Tremolo:

Master fingerstyle tremolo, a rapid repetition of a single note or a set of notes. This technique is common in classical guitar and can add intensity to your compositions.

Double Stops:

Incorporate double stops, playing two notes simultaneously, to create harmonies and intervals within your fingerstyle arrangements.

Campanella Technique:

Employ the campanella technique, where each note of a melody is played on a different string. This creates a cascading effect and a bell-like quality.

Hybrid Picking:

Combine fingerpicking with the use of a pick (hybrid picking). This technique allows for a versatile and dynamic approach, especially when playing both melody and chords.

Fingerstyle Tapping:

Experiment with tapping techniques using your fingers. This can involve tapping on the fretboard to produce percussive effects or tapping out melodies.

Rasgueado Technique:

Learn the flamenco-inspired rasgueado technique, which involves rapid strumming using multiple fingers. This technique adds flair and excitement to your compositions.

Cascading Arpeggios:

Create cascading arpeggios by playing arpeggiated chords in a descending or ascending fashion. This adds a sense of movement and flow to your fingerstyle compositions.

Remember to blend these techniques creatively, and adapt them to suit the mood and theme of your composition. Fingerstyle techniques offer a rich palette for self-expression, allowing you to convey a wide range of emotions and atmospheres in your guitar compositions.

HARMONICS

Experiment with natural and artificial harmonics. These ethereal sounds can be used to create shimmering, bell-like tones in your compositions.

HARMONIC EXPERIMENTATION

Experimenting with natural and artificial harmonics in guitar composition can add unique textures, ethereal tones, and interesting effects to your music.

NATURAL HARMONICS

Understanding Natural Harmonics:

Natural harmonics are produced by lightly touching the strings at specific nodal points while plucking. Commonly found at the 12th, 7th, and 5th frets, these harmonics create bell-like tones.

Harmonic Overtones:

Explore the harmonic overtones present on each string. Understanding the physics of harmonics can help you identify additional harmonic points on the fretboard, allowing for more creative possibilities.

Harmonic Chords:

Integrate natural harmonics into chord progressions. Use them as accents or as the focal points of certain chords to create a celestial and resonant quality.

Harmonic Cascades:

Create cascading harmonic passages by moving between different harmonic points. This technique adds movement and a shimmering quality to your compositions.

Combining Harmonics with Fingerstyle:

Combine natural harmonics with fingerstyle techniques. Use them within arpeggios, picking patterns, or chordal arrangements to enhance the overall sonic palette.

Dynamic Control:

Experiment with dynamic control when playing natural harmonics. Adjusting the pressure on the strings and the force of your plucking hand can influence the volume and sustain of the harmonics.

ARTIFICIAL HARMONICS

Creating Artificial Harmonics:

Artificial harmonics involve fretting a note with one hand and lightly touching the string with the other hand to produce a harmonic. This technique allows for greater control over the harmonic's pitch.

Pinch Harmonics:

Explore pinch harmonics by combining artificial harmonics with picking. This technique is commonly used in rock and metal genres, creating a sharp and expressive sound.

Harmonic Melodies:

Develop melodies using artificial harmonics. Experiment with intervals and scales to craft intricate and melodic passages that showcase the unique tonal qualities of artificial harmonics.

Harmonic Swells:

Incorporate harmonic swells by gradually applying pressure to the harmonic point. This technique can create a swelling or fading effect, adding a dynamic and atmospheric touch to your compositions.

Hybrid Techniques:

Combine artificial harmonics with other techniques such as slides, bends, or vibrato. This integration can result in expressive and unconventional sounds.

String Skipping:

Experiment with string skipping while playing artificial harmonics. This can lead to interesting intervals and sonic landscapes, especially when used in conjunction with unconventional fretting positions.

TIPS FOR WORKING WITH HARMONICS

Experiment with Different Strings:

Different strings may respond differently to harmonic techniques. Explore how natural and artificial harmonics sound on each string to find the most resonant and pleasing results.

Combine with Effects:

Enhance the harmonic textures by using effects like reverb, delay, and modulation. Experimenting with effects can add depth and character to your harmonic passages.

Think Spatially:

Consider the spatial placement of harmonics within your compositions. Utilize the stereo field or pan effects to create a sense of space and dimension.

Dynamic Range:

Pay attention to the dynamic range when incorporating harmonics. Varied dynamics can evoke different emotions and highlight the nuances of the harmonic content.

By embracing the versatility of natural and artificial harmonics, you can elevate your guitar compositions, adding a touch of magic and intrigue to your musical creations.

SLIDE GUITAR

Explore slide guitar techniques using a bottleneck or slide. This technique can infuse your compositions with a bluesy, soulful quality.

SLIDE GUITAR TECHNIQUES

Slide guitar techniques can introduce a distinctive and expressive element to your compositions. Whether you're playing blues, rock, country, or experimenting with various genres, incorporating slides can add a unique flavor to your music.

Understanding the Slide:

A slide, typically made of glass, metal, or ceramic, is worn on the finger. Sliding the slide along the strings creates a smooth and gliding effect, altering the pitch of the notes.

Slide Placement:

Experiment with slide placement. You can place the slide directly over the fret, between frets, or even above the fretboard for different tonal qualities. Each position produces distinct sounds, and sliding from one position to another can create expressive transitions.

Single Note Slides:

Start with single note slides. Slide into and out of notes for smooth and emotive phrasing. Practice controlling the pressure and speed of the slide to achieve the desired expressiveness.

Slide Vibrato:

Add vibrato to sustained notes by rocking the slide back and forth. This technique can infuse warmth and character into your melodies.

Double Stops and Chords:

Experiment with double stops (playing two notes simultaneously) and chords using the slide. Sliding into chord voicings can produce rich and soulful sounds, particularly in blues and folk genres.

Open Tunings:

Explore open tunings, which are popular for slide guitar. Common open tunings include Open D (DADF#AD), Open G (DGDGBD), and Open E (EBEG#BE). Open tunings can enhance resonance and make it easier to create slide-friendly chord shapes.

Slide Runs and Licks:

Develop slide runs and licks. Practice sliding between notes in scales, creating runs that add flair to your solos. Combine these runs with other techniques like bending and vibrato for a dynamic sound.

Damping and Muting:

Learn to control string noise. Slides can produce unwanted string noise, especially when moving between positions. Practice muting and damping techniques to keep your playing clean.

Slide Harmonics:

Experiment with creating harmonics using the slide. By lightly touching the string above specific frets while sliding, you can produce harmonic overtones for a haunting and atmospheric effect.

Fretless Neck Exploration:

If you're using a fretless guitar, take advantage of the entire neck. Slides on a fretless guitar offer more flexibility in pitch, allowing for microtonal expressions.

Dynamic Control:

Practice dynamic control with your picking hand. Adjusting the pressure and angle of the slide can influence the volume, sustain, and timbre of the notes.

Combining with Other Techniques:

Integrate slides with other techniques such as hammer-ons, pull-offs, and bending. This combination can result in a more versatile and expressive playing style.

Listening to Slide Players:

Listen to renowned slide guitarists across genres. Study their phrasing, slide techniques, and how they incorporate slides into their compositions. This can provide inspiration and insights into different stylistic approaches.

Experiment with Different Slides:

Try different materials and sizes for your slides. Each material produces unique tones, and experimenting with various slides can help you find the one that suits your playing style and desired sound.

Recording Considerations:

When recording slide guitar, experiment with microphone placement. Capturing the nuances of slide playing may require different mic positions to emphasize the slide sound and overall tone.

Incorporating slide guitar techniques into your compositions can unlock a world of expressive possibilities. Whether you're aiming for soulful blues, rootsy folk, or experimental sounds, the slide is a versatile tool that can infuse your music with emotion and character.

ALTERNATE PICKING AND TREMOLO

Use alternate picking and tremolo picking techniques to create dynamic and fast-paced passages. These techniques can add excitement and intensity to your compositions.

INCORPORATING ALTERNATE AND TREMOLO PICKING

Alternate picking and tremolo picking are two essential techniques that can add dynamism and energy to your guitar compositions. Mastering these techniques allows you to create fast, articulate passages and contribute to the overall expressiveness of your music.

ALTERNATE PICKING

Definition:

Alternate picking involves using a down-up motion with your picking hand to play individual notes. This technique helps achieve speed and precision.

Practice Exercises:

Begin with simple exercises, playing scales or single-note patterns.

Gradually increase speed while maintaining accuracy.

Practice alternate picking across strings and different frets to enhance coordination.

String Skipping:

Experiment with string skipping exercises to develop agility.

This technique adds a challenging dimension to your playing and helps you navigate the fretboard more efficiently.

Arpeggios and Chords:

Apply alternate picking to arpeggios and chord progressions for a dynamic and percussive sound.

Use this technique to articulate each note in a chord, creating clarity and definition.

Combining with Other Techniques:

Integrate alternate picking with other techniques such as hammer-ons, pull-offs, and slides to create diverse and expressive phrases.

Experiment with incorporating alternate picking into your lead and rhythm playing.

Dynamic Control:

Practice dynamic control by varying the intensity of your picking. This adds nuance to your playing, allowing you to convey different emotions.

Syncopation:

Experiment with syncopated rhythms using alternate picking. This creates a sense of unpredictability and groove in your compositions.

Applying to Different Genres:

Explore how alternate picking is used in various genres such as rock, metal, jazz, and classical music.

Adapt the technique to suit the stylistic requirements of your composition.

TREMOLO PICKING

Definition:

Tremolo picking involves rapidly alternating between two notes or more, creating a continuous, trembling effect. It's commonly used to build intensity and momentum.

Start Slow:

Begin with slow tremolo picking on a single note to develop control and precision.

Gradually increase the speed as you become more comfortable with the motion.

Scale Patterns:

Apply tremolo picking to scale patterns, emphasizing the speed and uniformity of the picking motion.

Experiment with ascending and descending runs to explore different tonal possibilities.

Chord Tremolo:

Experiment with tremolo picking on chords, especially in softer sections of your composition. This adds a shimmering quality to the sound.

Dynamic Variation:

Use dynamic variation in your tremolo picking. Start softly and gradually increase the intensity to create a climactic effect.

Experiment with abrupt dynamic changes for a more dramatic impact.

Combining with Sustained Notes:

Blend tremolo picking with sustained notes to create contrast and tension in your compositions.

This combination is effective for building anticipation before resolving into a new section.

Applying to Different Genres:

Explore how tremolo picking is used in genres like black metal, folk, and classical music.

Adapt the technique to fit the mood and atmosphere of your composition.

Experiment with Finger Placement:

Try tremolo picking closer to the bridge for a brighter tone or closer to the neck for a warmer sound.

Experimenting with different tonal qualities adds versatility to your playing.

PRACTICE TIPS

Metronome Practice:

Use a metronome to practice both alternate picking and tremolo picking. This helps develop a steady sense of timing and improves accuracy.

Isolated String Practice:

Focus on each string individually when practicing these techniques. This ensures that you can execute them cleanly across the entire fretboard.

Gradual Tempo Increase:

Gradually increase the tempo as you become more comfortable with these techniques. Consistent and incremental progress leads to better mastery.

Record and Analyze:

Record yourself practicing and listen back. This allows you to identify areas for improvement and track your progress.

Experiment with Articulation:

Experiment with varying degrees of articulation. This includes adjusting the attack and release of each note to create a more nuanced and expressive performance.

Mastering alternate picking and tremolo picking opens up a wide range of possibilities for dynamic and expressive guitar compositions. Whether you're aiming for speed and precision or creating tension and intensity, these techniques can significantly enhance your playing style. Regular practice and experimentation with these techniques will contribute to your growth as a versatile guitarist.

FRETBOARD TAPPING

Integrate fretboard tapping for percussive and rapid melodic sequences. This technique is commonly associated with progressive and fingerstyle guitar playing.

INTEGRATING FRETBOARD TAPPING

Fretboard tapping is a versatile technique that can add percussive and rapid melodic sequences to your guitar compositions. Popularized by guitarists like Eddie Van Halen and expanded upon by many others, tapping involves using your fingers to fret and sound notes on the fretboard, creating a distinctive and expressive sound.

BASICS OF FRETBOARD TAPPING

Hand Position:
For standard tapping, use your picking hand's fingers to tap the strings.

Position your tapping hand over the neck, perpendicular to the frets, allowing your fingers to easily reach the strings.

Finger Selection:
While any finger can be used for tapping, the index, middle, and ring fingers are commonly employed.

Experiment with different fingers to achieve varied tones and dynamics.

Hammer-Ons and Pull-Offs:

Tapping involves using hammer-ons and, sometimes, pull-offs to sound notes without picking.

Tap the string with sufficient force for a clean sound and then release to create a pull-off effect.

Combining with Picking:

Tapping is often combined with conventional picking. This allows for seamless transitions between tapped and picked notes, expanding your tonal palette.

Two-Handed Tapping:

Explore two-handed tapping, where both hands contribute to the tapping technique. This can result in complex and rapid sequences.

PERCUSSIVE SEQUENCES

Rhythmic Patterns:

Use tapping to create rhythmic patterns by tapping on and off the fretboard in sync with a beat.

Experiment with different rhythmic subdivisions to add variety to your sequences.

Percussive Elements:

Incorporate tapping as a percussive element by tapping on the strings lightly without fully fretting notes.

This adds a unique percussive layer to your composition.

Chordal Tapping:

Tap multiple notes simultaneously to create chordal sequences.

Experiment with arpeggios and unconventional chord shapes to expand your harmonic possibilities.

RAPID MELODIC SEQUENCES

Scale Runs:

Utilize tapping for fast scale runs. This technique can produce rapid, flowing melodic sequences.

Combine tapping with legato techniques like slides and hammer-ons for a smooth and fluid sound.

Intervallic Tapping:

Tap intervals or specific note combinations to create melodic interest.

Experiment with different intervals and note groupings for unique and expressive sequences.

String Skipping:

Incorporate tapping into string skipping patterns for a wider melodic range.

This technique can create intricate and dynamic melodic sequences.

Dynamic Control:

Vary the intensity of your taps to add dynamic contrast to your sequences.

Use different fingers and tapping locations for tonal variation.

PRACTICE TIPS

Start Slow:

Begin with slow, controlled tapping exercises to build accuracy and coordination.

Isolate Techniques:

Focus on specific tapping techniques, such as chordal tapping, percussive tapping, or two-handed tapping, during practice sessions.

Use a Metronome:

Practice tapping along with a metronome to develop precise timing and control at different tempos.

Experiment with Finger Combinations:

Explore different finger combinations for tapping to discover unique tones and textures.

Incorporate Tapping in Compositions:

Integrate tapping into your compositions gradually. Start with simpler sequences before progressing to more complex arrangements.

EXAMPLES

Percussive Sequence:

Create a rhythmic pattern by tapping lightly on muted strings, adding a percussive layer to your composition.

Melodic Sequence:

Construct a melodic sequence by tapping a descending arpeggio on the higher frets, combining it with legato techniques.

Chordal Tapping:

Experiment with tapping multiple notes simultaneously to create rich, chordal sequences.

Two-Handed Tapping:

Develop a two-handed tapping section where both hands contribute to intricate and rapid melodic phrases.

Fretboard tapping is a dynamic and expressive technique that, when mastered, can elevate your guitar compositions. By incorporating tapping into your repertoire, you add a layer of versatility and creativity to your playing style. As with any technique, regular practice, experimentation, and gradual integration into your compositions will contribute to your proficiency and musical expression.

DOUBLE STOPS AND BENDS

Incorporate double stops and bends to create expressive and emotive phrases. These techniques can add a vocal-like quality to your guitar lines.

INCORPORATING DOUBLE STOPS AND BENDS

Incorporating double stops and bends into your guitar composition can add expressive and emotive qualities, enriching your musical phrases with a wide range of dynamics. Both techniques provide opportunities to infuse your playing with emotion, allowing you to convey feelings ranging from subtle nuances to intense expressions.

DOUBLE STOPS

Definition:
Double stops involve playing two notes simultaneously, typically on adjacent strings.
They can be harmonized intervals (thirds, fifths, etc.) or notes from the same scale, creating a harmonically rich sound.

Techniques:
Experiment with various double stop techniques, such as sliding into double stops, hammering on or pulling off one of the notes, or incorporating muted strums for percussive effects.

Emotional Impact:

Double stops can evoke a sense of depth and emotion, making them ideal for conveying mood and feeling in your compositions.

Thirds and sixths often provide a sweet and harmonious quality, while fifths can introduce a robust and stable sound.

Melodic Integration:

Integrate double stops within melodic sequences to emphasize specific notes or create harmonically rich passages.

Use them as embellishments to highlight key moments in your composition.

Chordal Double Stops:

Explore double stops as a way to outline chords within your composition.

Experiment with different chord voicings and inversions to add color and variety.

BENDS

Definition:

Bending involves pushing or pulling a string across the fretboard to change the pitch of a note.

Bends can be whole, half, or quarter-tone bends, each offering a different expressive quality.

Techniques:

Practice both upward and downward bends to incorporate a variety of expressive gestures.

Combine bends with vibrato by oscillating the pitch of the bent note for added expressiveness.

Emotional Impact:

Bends are powerful tools for infusing emotion into your playing. A well-executed bend can convey tension, release, or even sadness.

Experiment with bending multiple notes simultaneously for a harmonically rich effect.

Varying Bend Speed:

The speed and smoothness of your bend can greatly influence its emotional impact.

Slow, controlled bends can build anticipation, while quick, aggressive bends can inject intensity.

Bend Releases:

Explore the expressive potential of releasing a bend gradually rather than returning to the original pitch immediately.

This technique adds a nuanced, emotive quality to your phrases.

COMBINING DOUBLE STOPS AND BENDS

Harmonic Texture:

Combine double stops and bends to create lush harmonic textures.

Experiment with bending one note of a double stop while keeping the other static for a unique tonal blend.

Expressive Phrasing:

Use double stops to punctuate melodic phrases and bends to add dynamic contour to your lines.

Employ bends and double stops strategically to enhance the emotional impact of key moments in your composition.

Unison Bends:

Perform unison bends where one note is fretted, and the other is bent to match its pitch. This creates a unified, expressive effect.

Experiment with different intervals for added versatility.

Dynamic Contrast:

Utilize the contrast between the sustained, harmonically rich sound of double stops and the dynamic pitch changes of bends to create expressive phrases with depth.

EXAMPLES

Soulful Double Stop Melody:

Incorporate double stops in a slow, soulful melody. Experiment with third and sixth intervals to evoke a contemplative mood.

Bending Blues Lick:

Create a bluesy lick by combining quarter-tone bends with double stops. Use a mix of major and minor pentatonic scales for emotional variety.

Chordal Double Stop Progression:

Develop a chord progression using chordal double stops. Experiment with bending one note of the double stop to introduce a subtle yet expressive touch.

Epic Solo with Bends and Double Stops:

Construct an epic guitar solo by combining fast, aggressive bends with strategically placed double stops. Use this to build tension and release throughout the solo.

In summary, incorporating double stops and bends into your guitar composition adds a layer of expressiveness and emotion to your playing. Experiment with different techniques, intervals, and stylistic approaches to discover the unique voice that these techniques can bring to your music.

The combination of double stops and bends offers a vast palette for creating compelling and emotive phrases, allowing you to convey a wide range of feelings in your guitar compositions.

SLAP AND POP

Adopt slap and pop techniques commonly associated with bass playing. This unconventional approach can bring a rhythmic and percussive element to your guitar compositions.

ADOPTING SLAP AND POP TECHNIQUES

Adopting slap and pop techniques in guitar composition can bring a percussive and dynamic dimension to your music. These techniques, commonly associated with bass guitar playing, involve striking the strings with your thumb (slap) and plucking or pulling them with your fingers (pop). When applied to the guitar, they can add rhythmic intensity, groove, and a funky feel.

SLAP TECHNIQUE

Thumb Positioning:
Position your thumb parallel to the strings, slightly above the one you intend to strike.

Aim for a percussive sound by hitting the strings with the fleshy part of your thumb.

Snap and Release:
Develop a snapping motion with your thumb, pulling it away from the strings immediately after striking.

This creates a sharp attack, producing the characteristic slap sound.

Experiment with Articulation:

Vary the intensity of your slap for different dynamics.

Experiment with slapping different parts of the strings to achieve varying tones.

Incorporate Ghost Notes:

Introduce ghost notes by lightly slapping the strings without fully engaging them.

This adds rhythmic complexity and groove to your compositions.

POP TECHNIQUE

Finger Plucking:

Use your fingers (usually index, middle, or both) to pluck or pull the strings after slapping.

Plucking can be done by snapping your fingers against the strings, producing a distinctive popping sound.

Experiment with Finger Placement:

Experiment with plucking near the neck for a warmer tone or closer to the bridge for a brighter, sharper sound.

Adjust the angle and force of your pluck to explore different timbres.

Combine Slaps and Pops:

Create rhythmic patterns by alternating between slaps and pops.

Develop syncopated rhythms and accents to enhance the groove in your composition.

Use Multiple Fingers:

Incorporate multiple fingers to pop strings simultaneously, creating chords or harmonies.

This technique adds richness and complexity to your compositions.

APPLYING SLAP AND POP IN COMPOSITION

Rhythmic Foundation:

Use slap and pop techniques to establish a rhythmic foundation for your composition.

Build a percussive groove that complements other rhythmic elements in your music.

Bassline Emulation:

Emulate the role of a bass guitar by incorporating slap and pop techniques into your basslines.

This is particularly effective in genres like funk, jazz, or fusion.

Funky Accents:

Introduce slap and pop accents to enhance the funkiness of specific phrases or chord progressions.

Experiment with unexpected rhythmic placements for added flair.

Dynamic Transitions:

Use slap and pop techniques to create dynamic transitions between different sections of your composition.

Gradually build intensity by incorporating more aggressive slapping or intricate popping patterns.

Soloing and Melodic Lines:

Explore using slap and pop in soloing to add flair to your melodic lines.

Combine slaps, pops, and conventional picking techniques for a diverse sonic palette.

EXAMPLES

Funky Rhythm Section:

Create a rhythmic foundation with slap and pop techniques, supporting your composition's rhythmic structure.

Slap Bass Solo:

Feature a slap bass solo within your composition, utilizing both techniques for a dynamic and expressive performance.

Chordal Slapping:

Develop chord progressions where slapping is incorporated to outline the rhythmic structure, while pops add melodic accents.

Slap and Pop Soloing:

Integrate slap and pop techniques into a guitar solo, blending them with traditional picking for a versatile and expressive performance.

In summary, adopting slap and pop techniques in your guitar composition opens up a world of rhythmic possibilities and adds a distinct flavor to your playing. Experiment with different approaches, rhythmic patterns, and dynamics to find creative ways to incorporate these techniques into your music. Whether you're aiming for a funky groove or a dynamic solo, slap and pop can be powerful tools for enhancing the overall character and energy of your guitar compositions.

PALM MUTING

Experiment with palm muting to control the sustain and create a staccato effect. This technique is effective for rhythmic and percussive playing.

UTILIZING PALM MUTING

Utilizing palm muting in guitar composition is a technique that involves using the fleshy part of your palm to lightly touch and dampen the strings near the bridge of the guitar. This technique is commonly employed to create a percussive and controlled sound, adding a unique texture to your playing.

PALM MUTING TECHNIQUE

Hand Placement:
Position your picking hand with the side of your palm lightly resting on the strings, close to the bridge.

Experiment with the exact placement to achieve the desired level of muting.

Pressure Control:
Apply just enough pressure to dampen the strings without fully blocking their vibration.

Adjust the pressure to control the degree of muting and achieve varying dynamics.

String Selection:
Palm muting is often more pronounced on lower strings, but it can be applied to any string.

Experiment with muting different strings to create diverse tonal textures.

Strumming and Picking:

Practice both strumming and picking while maintaining the palm muting technique.

Experiment with different strumming patterns and picking styles to find what works best for your composition.

APPLICATIONS IN COMPOSITION

Rhythmic Emphasis:

Use palm muting to emphasize specific beats or accents within your compositions.

This technique is effective for creating a tight and percussive feel in rhythm guitar parts.

Dynamics and Expression:

Gradually release or apply more pressure to the strings to introduce dynamics and expression.

Combine palm-muted sections with open, ringing chords for contrast and impact.

Chord Progressions:

Apply palm muting to individual chords or entire progressions to add a rhythmic, staccato quality.

Experiment with muting different chords within a progression for tonal variety.

Strumming Patterns:

Develop strumming patterns that incorporate palm muting for sections requiring a more controlled and subdued sound.

Transition between palm-muted and open strumming for dynamic contrast.

Single Note Lines:

Apply palm muting to single-note lines and melodies for a percussive, plucked effect.

This can be particularly effective in lead guitar parts where you want to add a rhythmic punch.

EXAMPLES

Verse Dynamics:

Use palm muting during verses to create a subdued and intimate atmosphere.

Transition to open strumming or picking in the chorus for a dynamic lift.

Power Chord Progressions:

Apply palm muting to power chord progressions for a heavy and rhythmic foundation.

Release the mute during climactic moments to enhance the impact.

Percussive Acoustic Strumming:

Employ palm muting in acoustic compositions for a percussive strumming effect.

Combine with open chords for a balance of dynamics.

Funky Riffs:

Incorporate palm muting into funky guitar riffs to achieve a tight and groovy sound.

Experiment with muted and unmuted sections for rhythmic variety.

TIPS

Experiment with Pressure:

Vary the pressure of your palm to explore different levels of muting.

Find the sweet spot that suits the mood and intensity of your composition.

Combine Techniques:

Combine palm muting with other techniques like slides, hammer-ons, and pull-offs to enhance expressiveness.

Experiment with how different techniques complement each other.

Use in Various Genres:

While often associated with rock and metal, palm muting can be applied to various genres, including acoustic, pop, and funk.

Adapt the technique to fit the style of your composition.

Practice Control:

Develop control over your palm muting technique through consistent practice.

Practice with a metronome to improve rhythmic precision.

Palm muting is a versatile technique that can add a rhythmic, percussive quality to your guitar compositions. Whether you're crafting dynamic chord progressions, rhythmic strumming patterns, or expressive lead lines, palm muting can be a valuable tool for shaping the overall feel and texture of your music. Experiment with different applications and incorporate this technique to enhance the rhythmic and dynamic elements of your guitar compositions.

HAMMER-ONS AND PULL-OFFS

Integrate hammer-ons and pull-offs for smooth and legato passages. These techniques enhance fluidity and can be used for quick, melodic runs.

INTEGRATION

Integrating hammer-ons and pull-offs in guitar composition is a technique that adds fluidity, expressiveness, and a legato quality to your playing. Hammer-ons involve sounding a note by "hammering" onto the fretboard with another finger, while pull-offs produce a note by pulling the finger off the fretboard to a lower fret.

HAMMER-ONS

Execution:
Play an initial note, then use a different finger to "hammer" onto a higher fret without picking again.
Ensure a firm, controlled hammering motion to produce a clear and sustained note.

Finger Placement:
Typically, use the index or middle finger for the initial note and the ring or pinky finger for the hammer-on.
Experiment with different finger combinations for varied tonal effects.

Application:
Use hammer-ons for embellishments, creating legato passages, or adding speed to your compositions.

PULL-OFFS

Execution:

Play a note, then lift the finger off the fret to sound the note on a lower fret without picking again.

Ensure a swift and controlled pull-off for clarity.

Finger Placement:

Generally, use the ring or pinky finger for the initial note and the index or middle finger for the pull-off.

Experiment with different finger combinations for different tonal textures.

Application:

Incorporate pull-offs for creating smooth transitions between notes, adding expressiveness to melodies, or executing fast, cascading runs.

APPLICATIONS IN COMPOSITION

Expressive Melodies:

Use hammer-ons and pull-offs to craft expressive and fluid melodic lines.

Experiment with incorporating these techniques in slower, emotive sections to enhance expressiveness.

Legato Phrasing:

Employ hammer-ons and pull-offs for legato phrasing, allowing notes to seamlessly flow into one another.

This technique is effective in creating smooth and connected musical passages.

Fast Runs and Solos:

Integrate hammer-ons and pull-offs in fast runs and solos to achieve speed and agility.

Combine with alternate picking for intricate and dynamic solo sections.

Chord Embellishments:

Enhance chord progressions by adding hammer-ons and pull-offs to individual notes within the chords.

Experiment with incorporating these techniques in both acoustic and electric guitar compositions.

Dynamic Variation:

Use hammer-ons and pull-offs to introduce dynamic variation within a composition.

Contrast these techniques with picked notes for a balanced and nuanced performance.

EXAMPLES

Acoustic Fingerstyle:

In fingerstyle compositions, use hammer-ons and pull-offs to create intricate and melodic patterns.

Experiment with incorporating these techniques in arpeggios and chord progressions.

Blues Licks:

Integrate hammer-ons and pull-offs in blues licks for expressive and soulful playing.

Combine with bending and sliding for a classic blues sound.

Metal Shredding:

Utilize fast and precise hammer-ons and pull-offs in metal compositions for shredding solos.

Experiment with incorporating these techniques in scale runs and arpeggios.

Jazz Lines:

Add sophistication to jazz compositions by using hammer-ons and pull-offs in intricate melodic lines.

Experiment with combining these techniques with jazz chords.

TIPS

Practice Control:

Develop control over your hammer-ons and pull-offs through dedicated practice.

Gradually increase speed and accuracy to achieve a smooth and controlled execution.

Experiment with Finger Combinations:

Try different finger combinations for hammer-ons and pull-offs to discover unique tonal qualities.

Adapt your finger choices based on the musical context.

Combine with Other Techniques:

Integrate hammer-ons and pull-offs with other techniques like slides, bends, and vibrato for a versatile and expressive playing style.

Experiment with combining techniques to create a signature sound.

Incorporate into Your Practice Routine:

Dedicate specific practice sessions to focus on hammer-ons and pull-offs.

Include these techniques in scale exercises, melodic patterns, and improvisation to strengthen your overall technique.

Incorporating hammer-ons and pull-offs into your guitar compositions adds a layer of expressiveness and versatility to your playing. Whether you're crafting melodic lines, solo sections, or embellishing chords, these techniques provide a range of creative possibilities. Practice diligently, experiment with different contexts, and discover how hammer-ons and pull-offs can elevate the musicality of your guitar compositions.

WHAMMY BAR (TREMOLO ARM)

If your guitar is equipped with a whammy bar, explore pitch bends, dives, and expressive vibrato. These techniques can add a dynamic and expressive quality to your playing.

WHAMMY BAR TECHNIQUES

Whammy bar techniques, also known as vibrato arms or tremolo bars, provide guitarists with a unique way to manipulate pitch and add expressive nuances to their compositions.

Standard Vibrato

Execution:

Apply subtle pitch modulation by gently moving the whammy bar up and down.

Use this technique to add a touch of vibrato to sustained notes or chords.

Application:

Enhance emotional passages and sustained notes with a subtle vibrato effect.

Dive Bombs:

Execution:

Quickly depress the whammy bar, causing a rapid decrease in pitch.

Release the bar to return to the original pitch.

Application:

Introduce intense and dramatic moments, particularly in rock and metal compositions.

Use dive bombs for climactic sections or transitions.

Upward Bends:

Execution:

Pull the whammy bar upwards to raise the pitch of notes or chords.

Application:

Create ascending pitch effects for added excitement in solos or transitions.

Experiment with combining upward bends with scale runs.

Harmonic Emulation:

Execution:

Apply subtle vibrato to natural or artificial harmonics using the whammy bar.

Application:

Achieve ethereal and otherworldly sounds, especially in ambient or experimental compositions.

Flutter:

Execution:

Produce a rapid fluttering effect by rapidly moving the whammy bar up and down.

Application:

Add a unique texture to sustained chords or create tension in specific musical passages.

Experiment with flutter in conjunction with other effects like delay and reverb.

Squeals and Screeches:

Execution:

Apply a combination of bends and quick releases on the whammy bar to produce squealing or screeching sounds.

Application:

Introduce aggressive and experimental elements, especially in heavy genres like metal.

Use sparingly for emphasis in specific musical contexts.

APPLICATIONS IN COMPOSITION

Solo Enhancements:

Integrate whammy bar techniques to elevate solo sections.

Experiment with dive bombs, upward bends, and vibrato for dynamic and expressive solos.

Transitions and Buildups:

Use whammy bar effects during transitions or buildups to create anticipation.

Combine upward bends with sustained chords for a soaring effect.

Ambient and Experimental Sounds:

Explore harmonic emulation and flutter techniques for ambient or experimental compositions.

Blend whammy bar effects with other atmospheric elements like delay and reverb.

Genre-Specific Emphasis:

Tailor whammy bar techniques to suit the genre of your composition.

Employ squeals and screeches in metal, while using subtle vibrato in softer genres.

Textural Additions:

Enhance the overall texture of your composition by incorporating whammy bar effects alongside other playing techniques.

Consider using whammy bar effects in conjunction with chord progressions for a dynamic impact.

TIPS

Subtlety Is Key:

While whammy bar techniques can add flair, use them judiciously to avoid overuse.

Subtle application can be just as impactful as more dramatic techniques.

Experiment with Amplification:

Explore the impact of whammy bar techniques through different amplification setups.

Adjust your settings to achieve the desired balance between clarity and distortion.

Combine with Other Effects:

Experiment with combining whammy bar techniques with other effects like delay, reverb, and distortion.

Create unique sonic landscapes by layering multiple effects.

Practice Control:

Develop control over the whammy bar for precise and intentional execution.

Practice with a metronome to ensure rhythmic accuracy, especially in faster passages.

Maintenance:

Regularly check and maintain your guitar's tremolo system to ensure smooth operation of the whammy bar.

Lubricate pivot points and keep the instrument in good condition.

Incorporating whammy bar techniques in your guitar compositions can provide a wide range of expressive possibilities. Whether you're aiming for subtle vibrato, dramatic dives, or experimental sounds, the whammy bar is a versatile tool for adding character and emotion to your playing. Experiment with different techniques, apply them contextually, and discover how the whammy bar can enhance the sonic palette of your guitar compositions.

HYBRID PICKING

Combine fingerpicking with flatpicking using hybrid picking. This technique allows for versatility and can be used to play intricate passages.

Combining Fingerpicking with Flatpicking using

HYBRID PICKING IN GUITAR COMPOSITION

Hybrid picking is a versatile technique that combines elements of both fingerstyle and flatpicking, allowing guitarists to achieve a unique and dynamic sound. Integrating fingerpicking with flatpicking through hybrid picking opens up a wide range of possibilities for guitar composition.

HYBRID PICKING TECHNIQUE

Fingerpick and Flatpick Integration:
Execution:
Hold a flatpick between your thumb and index or middle finger.
Use the remaining fingers to pluck the strings independently or in combination with the flatpick.
Application:
Achieve a combination of percussive strumming (flatpicking) and intricate melodic or harmonic nuances (fingerpicking).

Hybrid Picking Patterns:
Execution:
Develop patterns that involve both flatpicking and fingerpicking elements.

Experiment with alternating between flatpicked chords and fingerpicked arpeggios or melodic lines.

Application:

Create contrast and dynamics within your composition by seamlessly transitioning between different picking styles.

String Independence:

Execution:

Train your fingers for independent movement to pluck specific strings while flatpicking others.

Practice precision in targeting individual strings with your fingers.

Application:

Use this technique for intricate arrangements where certain strings need emphasis or specific melodic phrases.

APPLICATIONS IN COMPOSITION

Verse/Chorus Dynamics:

Employ hybrid picking during verses for fingerstyle delicacy, and switch to flatpicking for a more powerful chorus.

Create a sonic journey within the composition by altering picking styles based on the section.

Melodic Accompaniment:

Use hybrid picking to weave melodic lines into chord progressions.

Enhance the harmonic content of your composition by incorporating fingerpicked embellishments.

Rhythmic Texture:

Combine flatpicking for rhythmic strumming patterns with fingerpicking to introduce subtle rhythmic textures.

Experiment with variations in dynamics to add complexity to the rhythmic feel.

Solo Sections:

Utilize hybrid picking in solo sections to achieve both speed and articulation.

Incorporate flatpicked runs with fingerpicked notes to create a diverse and expressive solo.

Fingerstyle Intros/Outros:

Begin or conclude your composition with fingerstyle intros or outros, providing a soft and introspective feel.

Transition seamlessly into flatpicking for the body of the composition.

TIPS

Balance and Control:

Strive for a balanced sound between flatpicking and fingerpicking elements.

Develop control to switch between the techniques smoothly.

Finger Strength and Independence:

Strengthen the fingers involved in hybrid picking to ensure clear and defined notes.

Practice exercises that enhance finger independence for precise picking.

Experiment with Finger Combinations:

Explore different finger combinations for hybrid picking, such as thumb and middle finger or thumb and ring finger.

Find combinations that suit your playing style and the demands of your composition.

Use in Various Genres:

Hybrid picking is versatile and can be applied to various genres, including folk, rock, country, and blues.

Experiment with adapting the technique to match the genre and mood of your composition.

Dynamic Expression:

Use hybrid picking to convey different emotions and expressions within your composition.

Experiment with picking intensity and fingerstyle nuances to evoke the desired mood.

In summary, combining fingerpicking with flatpicking using hybrid picking provides a rich palette of tonal possibilities for guitar composition. This technique allows you to seamlessly blend the percussive power of flatpicking with the expressive subtleties of fingerstyle playing. Through careful integration, you can enhance the overall musicality of your compositions, creating a unique and engaging listening experience. Practice regularly, experiment with various patterns, and let hybrid picking become a valuable tool in your creative arsenal.

NATURAL AND ARTIFICIAL PERCUSSION

Utilize the guitar as a percussive instrument by incorporating tapping on the body, slapping the strings, or creating rhythmic patterns with your hands.

INCORPORATING NATURAL AND ARTIFICIAL PERCUSSION IN GUITAR COMPOSITION

Adding percussion elements to your guitar compositions can greatly enhance rhythm, dynamics, and overall musicality. Both natural and artificial percussion techniques provide a rhythmic foundation that complements your guitar playing.

NATURAL PERCUSSION TECHNIQUES

Body Percussion:

Execution:

Use your hands to strike different parts of the guitar's body, such as the top, sides, or back.

Experiment with varied strikes, including taps, slaps, and knocks.

Application:

Introduce percussive beats that synchronize with your playing.

Enhance rhythmic complexity by incorporating body percussion during instrumental breaks.

Tap-and-Play:

Execution:

Combine fingerpicking or strumming with taps on the guitar's body.

Tap with your fingertips or nails for distinct percussive sounds.

Application:

Create syncopated rhythms by tapping on off-beats.

Use tap-and-play techniques to simulate a drumming effect while maintaining melodic elements.

Palm Muting:

Execution:

Rest the edge of your palm lightly on the strings near the bridge while strumming or picking.

Adjust the pressure for varying levels of muting.

Application:

Achieve a percussive, muted effect that works well in rhythmic passages.

Experiment with palm muting to accentuate specific beats or create a staccato feel.

ARTIFICIAL PERCUSSION TECHNIQUES

String Slaps and Snaps:

Execution:

Lift and release a string to produce a percussive slap against the fretboard.

Experiment with snapping the strings against the frets for a sharper sound.

Application:

Use string slaps to punctuate transitions between chords or sections.

Incorporate snaps for rhythmic emphasis, adding a crisp percussive layer.

Snare Drum Effect:

Execution:

Simulate a snare drum sound by striking the strings near the soundhole with your fingernails.

Experiment with different angles and intensity for varied snare effects.

Application:

Introduce a snare drum-like backbeat to complement the rhythm.

Use the snare effect to highlight specific beats within a measure.

Tapping and Knocking:

Execution:

Tap on the guitar's body or soundboard with your fingertips or knuckles.

Explore different areas to produce varied percussive tones.

Application:

Integrate tapping and knocking for accents, creating a diverse rhythmic palette.

Incorporate these techniques during instrumental breaks or to mark the beginning of a new section.

COMBINING NATURAL AND ARTIFICIAL PERCUSSION

Layering Techniques:

Combine body percussion, tapping, and string slaps to create layered percussive effects.

Experiment with different combinations to find a balance that complements your composition.

Dynamic Control:

Adjust the intensity of percussive elements based on the overall dynamics of your composition.

Use lighter percussion during softer sections and increase intensity for climactic moments.

Rhythmic Patterns:

Develop rhythmic patterns that synchronize natural and artificial percussion with your guitar playing.

Create patterns that enhance the groove and rhythm of your composition.

Transitions and Breaks:

Utilize percussion during transitions between sections to add excitement and maintain momentum.

Introduce breaks where the guitar takes a brief pause, allowing percussive elements to shine.

RECORDING CONSIDERATIONS

Microphone Placement:

Experiment with microphone placement to capture the nuances of both guitar playing and percussion.

Consider using multiple microphones to capture different aspects of the sound.

Balancing Levels:

When recording, ensure a balanced mix between guitar and percussion elements.

Pay attention to the volume levels to prevent percussive elements from overpowering the guitar.

PRACTICE TIPS

Isolation Exercises:

Practice percussive techniques in isolation to develop precision and control.

Focus on producing consistent and clear percussive sounds.

Metronome Practice:

Practice percussive elements with a metronome to develop a strong sense of timing.

Gradually increase the tempo to challenge your rhythmic abilities.

The integration of natural and artificial percussion in guitar composition adds depth, rhythm, and a unique dimension to your music. Experiment with different techniques, find ways to seamlessly blend percussive elements with your guitar playing, and let your creativity guide you in creating engaging and dynamic compositions.

USING EFFECTS CREATIVELY

Experiment with various guitar effects, such as reverb, delay, and modulation, to enhance the sonic landscape of your compositions.

EXPLORING CREATIVE USES OF VARIOUS GUITAR EFFECTS

Guitar effects are tools that can transform your sound, adding depth, texture, and ambiance to your compositions.

Reverb:
Effect: Creates a sense of space by simulating reflections in a room.

Creative Use:

Apply subtle reverb to create a natural room ambiance.

Experiment with long decay times for ethereal, atmospheric sounds.

Use spring reverb for vintage or surf-inspired tones.

Delay:
Effect: Replicates the original sound with repetitions.

Creative Use:

Create rhythmic patterns by syncing delay time with the song's tempo.

Experiment with short delays for slap-back effects.

Use ambient delays for a spacious, otherworldly feel.

Chorus:
Effect: Modifies the sound by doubling and detuning it.

Creative Use:
Add subtle chorus for a thicker, more expansive sound.
Use pronounced chorus settings for a shimmering, 80s-inspired tone.
Combine chorus with distortion for unique textures.

Phaser:
Effect: Modifies the sound by shifting the phase of the audio signal.
Creative Use:
Create swirling, dynamic textures with a slow phaser speed.
Apply faster settings for a pronounced, "jet plane" effect.
Use in conjunction with clean tones for a psychedelic touch.

Flanger:
Effect: Similar to a phaser but with a more pronounced sweeping effect.
Creative Use:
Employ gentle flanging for a subtle, spacey quality.
Intensify the effect for dramatic sweeps reminiscent of electric planes.
Combine with distortion for a unique, metallic character.

Tremolo:
Effect: Alters volume at a regular rate, creating a pulsating effect.

Creative Use:

Use slow tremolo for a subtle, throbbing ambiance.

Apply faster settings for a pronounced, rhythmic pulse.

Combine with reverb for a vintage, surf-inspired sound.

Distortion/Overdrive:

Effect: Adds gain and saturation, altering the guitar's natural tone.

Creative Use:

Use mild overdrive for a warm, bluesy tone.

Apply high-gain distortion for heavy, aggressive sounds.

Experiment with stacking overdrive and distortion pedals for unique textures.

Wah-Wah:

Effect: Modifies the tone by emphasizing certain frequencies.

Creative Use:

Create expressive, vocal-like sounds by manipulating the pedal.

Use dynamically for wah-infused solos.

Experiment with half-cocked positions for unique tonal variations.

Octaver:

Effect: Adds octaves above or below the original pitch.

Creative Use:

Generate thick, organ-like sounds by adding an octave below.

Experiment with octave-up settings for a unique lead tone.

Combine with distortion for synth-like textures.

Pitch Shifter:

Effect: Alters the pitch of the guitar signal.

Creative Use:

Create harmonies by shifting the pitch up or down.

Experiment with pitch shifting in real-time for dynamic effects.

Combine with delay for lush, ambient textures.

Vibrato:

Effect: Modifies pitch by oscillating it rapidly.

Creative Use:

Apply subtle vibrato for a touch of expressiveness.

Use faster settings for a pronounced, warbly effect.

Experiment with vibrato in conjunction with other modulation effects.

Looper:

Effect: Records and plays back a segment of your playing.

Creative Use:

Create layered compositions by recording and looping different parts.

Use loopers for on-the-fly accompaniment during live performances.

Experiment with creating evolving textures through layered loops.

TIPS FOR CREATIVE EXPLORATION:

Stacking Effects:

Combine multiple effects to discover unique sonic landscapes.

Experiment with different signal chain configurations for diverse textures.

Dynamic Playing:

Adjust effect parameters in real-time for dynamic expressiveness.

Use foot expression pedals to control parameters like volume, wah, or pitch.

Experiment with Settings:

Don't hesitate to tweak effect settings to find your unique sound.

Explore unconventional settings for unexpected and innovative results.

Contextual Application:

Consider the musical context when applying effects.

Use effects to enhance specific sections or create contrast within a composition.

Recording Techniques:

Experiment with microphone placement when recording to capture the nuances of your effects.

Use stereo configurations for wider spatial effects.

Live Performance:

Practice using effects seamlessly for live performances.

Incorporate effects judiciously to enhance the overall musical experience.

By exploring the creative potential of various guitar effects, you can personalize your sound, experiment with different genres, and elevate your guitar compositions to new heights. Embrace the experimentation process, and let your imagination guide you in crafting a sonic identity that is uniquely yours.

EMBRACING THE SYMPHONY WITHIN

As we draw the final curtains on our journey through the intricate labyrinth of creative guitar composition, it's time to reflect on the vast tapestry of knowledge and skill that we've woven together. From the foundational understanding of basic chord theory to the exploration of advanced techniques and effects, Storytelling With Sound: Fundamentals Of Creative Guitar Composition has served as our compass, guiding us through the depths of musical expression.

In our exploration, we've delved into the very essence of harmony, dissecting chord progressions with a surgeon's precision and breathing life into melodies with every strum and pluck. We've traversed through different keys, unlocking the doors to a myriad of musical landscapes, each with its own unique allure and charm.

From the humble beginnings of open and barre chords to the intricate dance of chord inversions and extensions, we've sculpted our sonic palette with care and finesse, crafting suspended and altered chords that whisper secrets of emotion and tension. We've danced along the edges of diatonic and non-diatonic realms, embracing chromatic movements that add depth and color to our compositions.

In our quest for musical mastery, we've embraced the power of experimentation, letting curiosity be our guide as we push the boundaries of rhythm, melody, and harmony. We've listened intently to the voices of other musicians, drawing inspiration from their wisdom and experience, and documenting our own musical adventures along the way.

As we stand at the threshold of this closing chapter, let us not forget the importance of staying playful and curious, of allowing our creativity to flow freely without fear or inhibition. Let us remember that every note we play is a brushstroke on the canvas of our sonic landscape, each rhythm a heartbeat in the symphony of life.

And so, dear reader, as you bid farewell to these pages and embark on your own musical odyssey, remember that the journey is just beginning. Let your fingers dance upon the fretboard with the grace of a poet, let your melodies soar like birds in flight, and let the sound of your guitar be the voice of your soul.

For in the end, it is not the destination that matters, but the beauty of the journey itself. And may your journey be filled with endless inspiration, boundless creativity, and the timeless magic of storytelling with sound.

Index

THANK YOU for purchasing Storytelling With Sound: Fundamentals of Creative Guitar Composition by University Scholastic Press. If you liked this book, please consider spreading your good word!

University Scholastic Press is an internationally renowned publisher and press, writing and producing textbooks, study guides, quote books, workbooks, cookbooks, journals, planners and creative nonfiction novels.

With offices in New York, London and Rome, University Scholastic Press is the trusted leader in producing and writing classic, bestselling books with an original, polished spin.

Other Musician's Series Books
By University Scholastic Press:

A Guitarist's Grimoire: Unlocking the Secrets of Creating A Musical Diary To Master Guitar Composition

Storytelling With Sound: Fundamentals of Creative Guitar Composition

Musical Architecture Secrets: Structure Planning For Guitar Composition

Strings Of Brilliance: Mastering Melody and Harmony Development For Guitar Composition

Rhythm Mastery for Guitarists: Unlocking Tempo and Timing Techniques For Guitar Composition